A Homeowner's Guide to Storage

A STACK OF CLEAN CLOTHES is piled on the bedroom chair because there isn't room for it in the crammed closet. The recycling is becoming a tripping hazard in the far corner of the kitchen. Spare toiletries are hidden away in the back of a hallway closet because the vanity is too small. Most of us have at least one room in our house that doesn't look or work the way we'd like (and let's be honest, most of us have more than one). We dream of our perfect house, our next house, which has all the space we need. But instead of dreaming of our next house, it's time to make our current space work better.

Nothing improves the feeling and function of a home like well-planned storage. Storage and organization projects allow us to make our spaces feel and function like much larger ones, and built-ins add instant value to any space without breaking the budget.

With the right tools and the right knowledge, you can tackle any disorganized room with confidence. STANLEY® has the tools, and with this *Homeowner's Guide* you'll get all of the design and how-to information needed to take your home from cluttered and ill-planned to functional and beautiful.　　　　　—Editors of *Fine Homebuilding*

STANLEY®
Built-ins and Storage

Editor: Christina Glennon
Copy Editor: Diane Sinitsky
Design and layout: Stacy Wakefield-Forte
Photographer: All photos and illustrations by Taunton Press staff
© The Taunton Press, Inc., except where noted.

The following names/manufacturers appearing in *Built-ins and Storage* are trademarks: Accuride®; Benjamin Moore®; Blum®; Enkamat®; Fastcap®; Häfele®; Marmoleum®; Minwax®; Rev-A-Shelf®; Rockler®; Sherwin-Williams®; Woodcraft®

FineHomebuilding

To contact us:
Fine Homebuilding
The Taunton Press
63 South Main Street, PO Box 5506,
Newtown, CT 06470-5506
Tel: 203-426-8171

Send an email: fh@taunton.com

Visit: www.finehomebuilding.com

To subscribe or place an order:
Visit www.finehomebuilding.com/fhorder
or call: 800-888-8286
9am-9pm ET Mon-Fri; 9am-5pm ET Sat

The Taunton guarantee:
If at any time you're not completely satisfied with *Fine Homebuilding*, you can cancel your subscription and receive a full and immediate refund of the entire subscription price. No questions asked.

T The Taunton Press
Inspiration for hands-on living®

CONTENTS

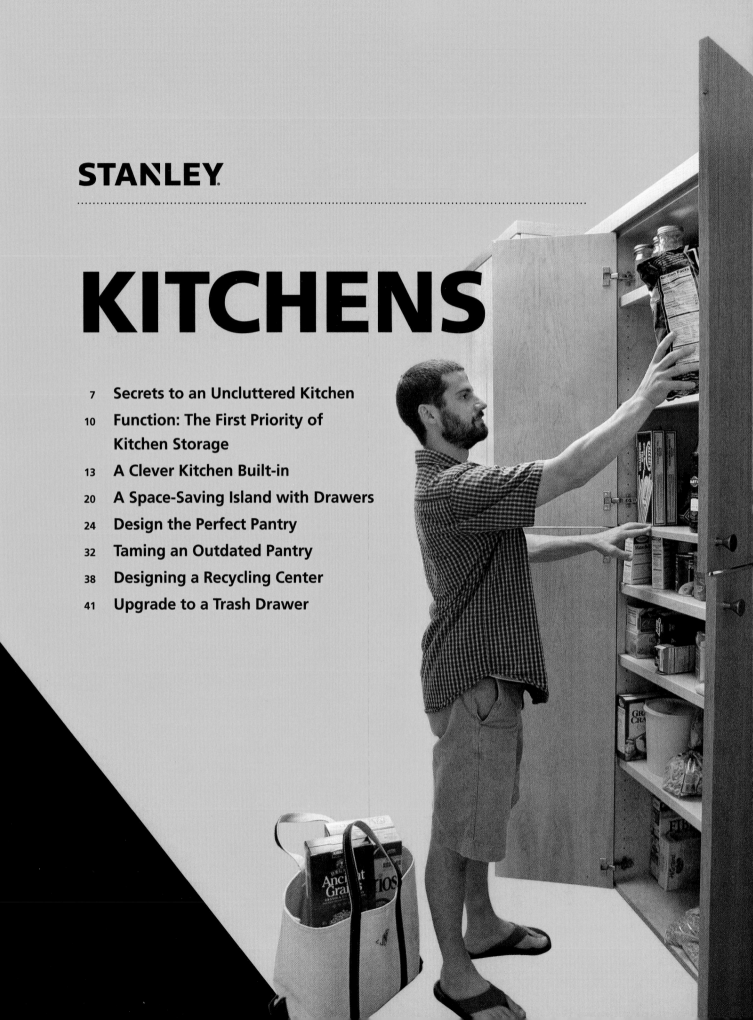

STANLEY

KITCHENS

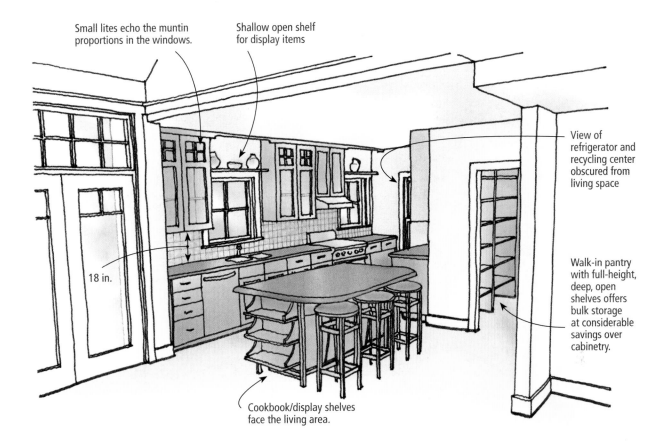

Small lites echo the muntin proportions in the windows.

Shallow open shelf for display items

View of refrigerator and recycling center obscured from living space

18 in.

Walk-in pantry with full-height, deep, open shelves offers bulk storage at considerable savings over cabinetry.

Cookbook/display shelves face the living area.

Secrets to an Uncluttered Kitchen

BY KATIE HUTCHISON One of the highest compliments I've ever been paid came from my 6-year-old nephew after he walked through our living and dining rooms into the kitchen and asked, "Where's all your stuff?"

Believe me, it's there—just not in plain sight.

Our living quarters and kitchen are small, so squirreling things away is a necessity, but large, open kitchens can benefit from the same storage strategies as small ones. To preserve or create a sense of spaciousness, stuff needs to be discreetly gathered and stowed.

Because large, open kitchens and small kitchens have unique storage challenges, I'll explore examples of both types in detail. The best solutions offer efficient, unobtrusive, appealing storage options that enhance kitchen function, flow, and feel. And they don't have to cost a lot.

If custom inset cabinets are out of reach, consider combining custom surrounds or dividers with stock, infill, overlay cabinets. Aligning the face of the surrounds or dividers with the face of the stiles and rails on the cabinet doors and drawers creates the illusion of inset cabinetry. Extending dividers for base cabinets to the floor creates "legs" between cabinets, enhancing the furniturelike look.

Limit cabinets in large, open kitchens

Some say that if you have a basement, no matter how big, you'll manage to fill it with your belongings. Large kitchens run the same risk. The trick is to keep a large kitchen, especially one that's part of an open plan, light and airy rather than filling it with cabinetry.

LARGE, OPEN KITCHEN

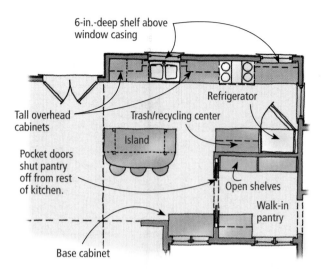

6-in.-deep shelf above window casing

Tall overhead cabinets

Pocket doors shut pantry off from rest of kitchen.

Island

Refrigerator

Trash/recycling center

Open shelves

Walk-in pantry

Base cabinet

To reinforce an expansive feel, leave ample room for windows and minimize overhead cabinets. In this example (drawing above), relegating much of the storage out of sight allows the island to float without overhead cabinets or a dividing storage wall between it and the living space.

SMALL KITCHEN (SINK WALL)

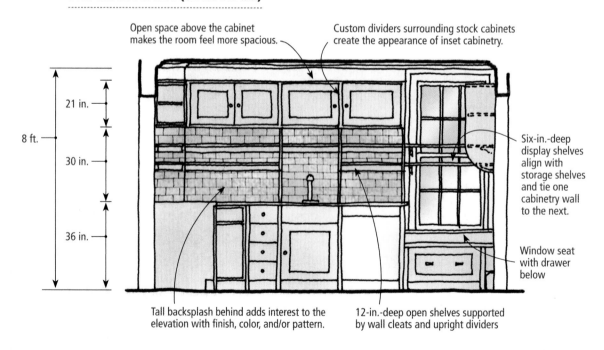

Open space above the cabinet makes the room feel more spacious.

Custom dividers surrounding stock cabinets create the appearance of inset cabinetry.

8 ft.

21 in.

30 in.

36 in.

Six-in.-deep display shelves align with storage shelves and tie one cabinetry wall to the next.

Window seat with drawer below

Tall backsplash behind adds interest to the elevation with finish, color, and/or pattern.

12-in.-deep open shelves supported by wall cleats and upright dividers

SMALL KITCHEN (OVERHEAD VIEW)

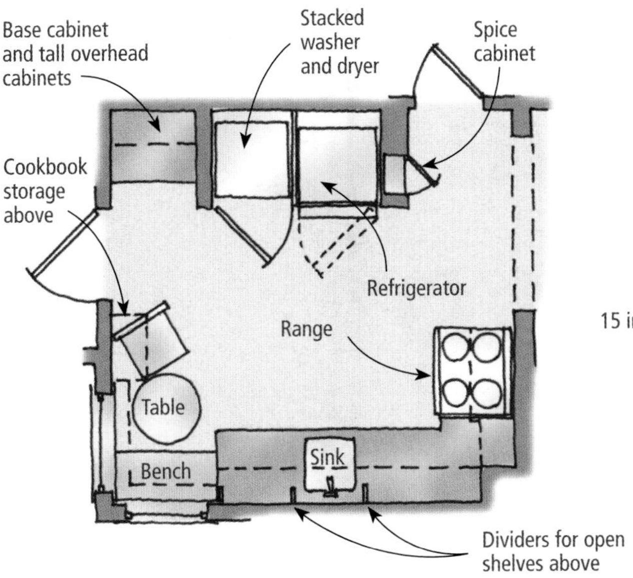

Base cabinet and tall overhead cabinets

Stacked washer and dryer

Spice cabinet

Cookbook storage above

Refrigerator

Range

Table

Bench

Sink

Dividers for open shelves above

SMALL KITCHEN (OPPOSITE WALL)

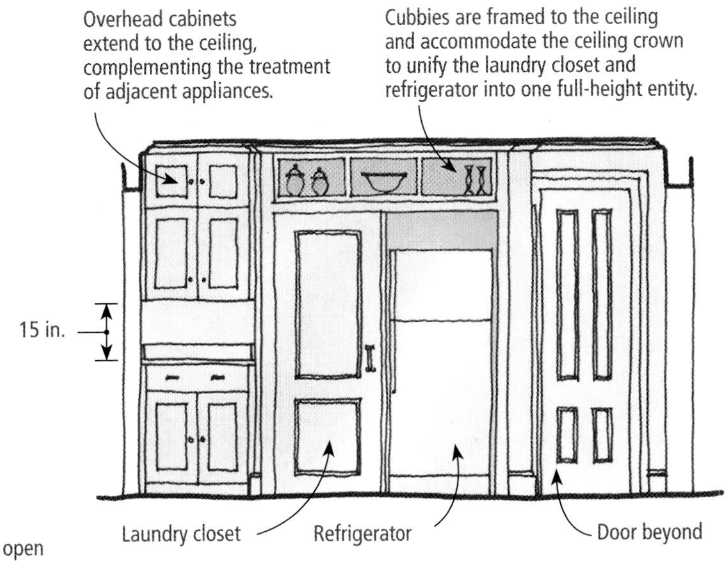

Overhead cabinets extend to the ceiling, complementing the treatment of adjacent appliances.

Cubbies are framed to the ceiling and accommodate the ceiling crown to unify the laundry closet and refrigerator into one full-height entity.

15 in.

Laundry closet

Refrigerator

Door beyond

Tuck bulk storage—including the refrigerator—and pantry space off the end of the kitchen that is most remote from open living spaces.

A tall pantry cabinet can abut the refrigerator, or as in this example, a base cabinet with tall overheads can serve a similar function. Because their contents are mostly out of view, the tall overheads don't need doors here. Large baskets or bins can be used without doors in this out-of-sight area as well, providing a welcome break from monolithic cabinetry.

Cabinets visible from the living space can be dressier. Glass-fronted overhead cabinets contribute to a more open look than opaque doors. Simple 6-in.-deep shelves above the windows provide display space.

Layers of storage work in a small kitchen

Storage in a small kitchen with a circulation path through the middle doesn't have to be inadequate or overbearing. With close attention to a functional layout and cabinet density and height, even a 138-sq.-ft. kitchen provides sufficient storage without feeling confined or cluttered.

On the sink wall, a combination of short overhead cabinets and open shelves meets a variety of storage needs.

Holding the top of the cabinets 9 in. below the ceiling gives the room a greater sense of spaciousness than if the cabinets were extended to the ceiling. The opaque fronts on the overhead cabinets conceal food packaging and less attractive wares, while the open shelves offer easy access to everyday glassware and china unlikely to gather dust due to frequent use. The 12-in.-deep shelves below the upper cabinets are supported by upright dividers that taper to 4 in. deep at the counter. The uprights continue the vertical lines of the base cabinet uprights, neatly organizing the sink wall. The shelves add a custom touch and a location to display attractive kitchenware at a fraction of the cost of cabinetry. The width of the uprights between the cabinets can account for differences between the length of a wall and stock-cabinet dimensions.

Shown above is the opposite wall, where the largest appliances are placed farthest from view. This wall bundles together the refrigerator and stackable washer and dryer, the tallest and deepest appliances. Cubbies above them take advantage of storage potential while keeping a more open feel than closed overhead cabinets would.

Katie Hutchison is an architect, design writer, and fine-art photographer in Warren, R.I. Her book *The New Small House* (The Taunton Press) will be available in October. Illustrations by the author.

Function: the First Priority of Kitchen Storage

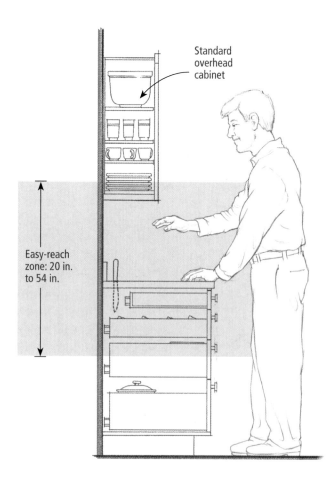

Standard overhead cabinet

Easy-reach zone: 20 in. to 54 in.

BY SAM CLARK The modern study of kitchen design began with the work of industrial engineers Frank and Lillian Gilbreth in the 1930s and continued with the Cornell Kitchen Study of the early 1950s. In their work-center concept, the Gilbreths said that kitchen work should be organized into distinct cleanup, cooking, and food-prep areas.

NOT ALL STORAGE IS GOOD STORAGE

Frequently used items should be accessible to most people. Store them in the top two drawers of the base cabinet and the bottom shelf of the upper cabinet. Storing knives in a countertop slot or knife block rather than a drawer eliminates several retrieval steps.

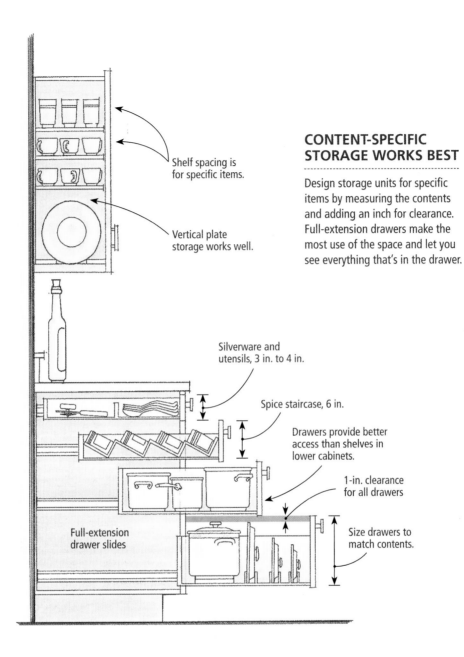

Shelf spacing is for specific items.

Vertical plate storage works well.

CONTENT-SPECIFIC STORAGE WORKS BEST

Design storage units for specific items by measuring the contents and adding an inch for clearance. Full-extension drawers make the most use of the space and let you see everything that's in the drawer.

Silverware and utensils, 3 in. to 4 in.

Spice staircase, 6 in.

Drawers provide better access than shelves in lower cabinets.

1-in. clearance for all drawers

Full-extension drawer slides

Size drawers to match contents.

Early design pioneers also developed effective principles for making each center efficient. Fifty years later, these principles are still useful, and surprisingly, they're still often ignored.

Reduce motions

First, store kitchen items at the point of first use. Most people store things by category: knives with knives and bowls with bowls. But if you use your paring knife at the sink and your carving knife near the stove, you should store each in the appropriate work center. Also, give premium positions to the most-used items.

Second, visualize the motions involved in using each item. If my favorite knife is in a drawer, I have to step back, grasp the drawer handle, pull open the drawer, find the right knife, take it out, and close the drawer. But if my knife is in a slot at the back of the counter, I can grab it, and I'm ready to go. That's the ideal: one-motion storage. If you study the motions for key kitchen tasks, you can design the storage that works best.

The area just above the counter, or the margin, is some of the most visible, convenient storage. Put shallow, open shelves or pot hooks here. If upper cabinets are necessary, position them 15 in. or less from the counter.

Windows to let in light are better than storage that people can't reach.

Margin area

Spices and utensils are kept where they are used frequently and are easy to find.

The easy-reach zone

Put the things you use the most in a region that almost anyone of any height, including wheelchair users, can reach easily. The accessible storage area for wheelchair users extends from knee level, perhaps 20 in. from the floor, to 44 in. or 48 in. up. For the able-bodied, I extend this easy-reach zone to 54 in. high, encompassing the top two drawers or upper shelves of the base cabinet, the space directly above the counter, and the first shelf of upper cabinets, if they are positioned relatively low.

Storage should be specific to contents

Shelves should be sized and spaced for the items they will hold. If a shelf is for 6-in.-tall cans, make the shelves 7 in. high at the most, which leaves clearance for access. (Measure the height of each drawer's contents, and add 1 in. Top drawers for utensils often can be as shallow as 3½ in.) By designing storage space to suit its contents, you can store much more in the optimum-reach zone.

Drawers work best in base cabinets

Although drawer cabinets cost more than door cabinets, they are worth the premium. A door cabinet is dark inside, and much of the volume goes unused. You have to lean or stoop to find things, and items in the back are blocked.

Drawers with good full-extension hardware can be packed front to back. Almost anything can be stored in drawers, including spices, knives, lids, large pots, small appliances—even a trash can or compost bucket.

Trash and compost

Locate the trash can as carefully as you would a major appliance. It should be near the sink, yet handy to the food-prep center. Use a pullout or a can with a foot pedal. My favorite detail has a top drawer with a stainless-steel bin for compost. Scraps can be swept directly into it from the chopping counter. Below it is the trash. Both pullouts fit easily in a 12½-in.-wide cabinet.

Sam Clark designs and builds kitchens in Plainfield, Vt. He is the author of *Remodeling a Kitchen* (The Taunton Press, 2003) and *The Independent Builder* (Chelsea Green, 1996). His website is www.samclarkdesign.com. Illustrations by Chuck Lockhart.

A Clever Kitchen Built-in

BY NANCY R. HILLER Modern kitchens are made for storage, but it never seems to be sufficient. Recently, my company built a cabinet to provide generous storage on a shallow section of wall in our clients' kitchen. It was space that normally would have gone to waste because it was too shallow for stock cabinets.

The inspiration for this custom-made cabinet came from a traditional piece of British furniture known as a Welsh dresser. In use since the 17th century, the dresser originally provided the main storage in a kitchen; built-in cabinets did not become the norm until the early 20th century. More commonly known in the United States by the less-elegant term hutch, the dresser typically has a shallow, open upper section that sits on a partially enclosed base. The dresser described here also exemplifies the sort of planning, production, and installation essential for genuinely custom built-in cabinets.

A strategy for storage

The kitchen had a section of unused wall about 11 ft. long, which I thought could be used for storage and display space without impeding traffic flow. Although 1 ft. of depth is shallow for a base cabinet, it is enough to hold a surprising variety of kitchen wares: cookbooks, decorative china, coffee mugs, small mixing bowls, jars of beans or pasta. Knowing that one of my clients had grown up in England and would be familiar with Welsh dressers, I suggested a similar cabinet with more-contemporary lines, customized for her family's budget and for the available space.

The upper sections would have open shelves, but the base cabinets would be enclosed with doors and drawers to keep their contents free of the dust and debris that collect at a kitchen's edges. Enclosing the lower sections also would give a nice visual weight to the wall without making it appear too heavy. The break between base and upper cabinets would be at 32 in., not the typical kitchen-counter height of 36 in., because I wanted this piece to look more like furniture than a regular kitchen cabinet.

Smaller components are easier

The six-piece unit is divided into three uppers and three bases for ease of production, delivery, and installation. To make the six plywood cases and the solid-maple counter

MORE PARTS MAKE CONSTRUCTION EFFICIENT

This type of modular cabinet construction allows a majority of the assembly work to be done in the shop. Consequently, I get more control over the processes and their costs.

resemble a single piece of cabinetry, I used a complete maple face frame on the center section of the upper and lower casework and a partial face frame on each end. The end cases would butt tightly against the center unit and share its face-frame stiles to make the unit appear as one piece.

Although 10-in. slides are available for many purposes and would have been ideal for this job, they are rated only for drawers up to approximately 2 ft. wide. For smooth operation, I needed hardware designed for oversize openings. Given the location of the adjacent door casing, which limited the cabinet's depth to a maximum of 12¾ in., and a design that called for inset drawer faces, we needed to create ¼ in. of additional depth to accommodate the 12-in. slides by routing out the plywood cabinet back in those locations.

For ease of production, I typically use a full-width applied back on built-in cabinets rather than rabbeting the cabinet sides to accept the back. Scribed on site, a finished end covers the seam between the cabinet and the ¼-in. back. After cutting biscuit slots to join the case sides to the tops, I used cleats fastened with glue and brads or screws to support the case bottoms. The biscuit- and cleat-supported butt joints were reinforced with 1½-in. screws once the casework was put together.

As we assembled the cases, I checked for square and twist. I also cleaned off squeezed-out glue before it dried.

Solid-wood parts need consideration

Depending on the finish, I use either mortise-and-tenon joinery or pocket screws to assemble face frames before gluing them to carcases. Although pocket screws are quick and simple, I don't think the joint is as immobile as a glued mortise and tenon. While a hairline gap isn't as noticeable in natural wood, I've learned the hard way not to use pocket screws for painted work that needs to look seamless. For this project, once the face frames were pocket-screwed, we glued and clamped them to the carcases.

The solid-maple counter was made by edge-joining two or three full-length boards. To increase the glue surface and to keep the boards even during clamping, I used biscuit joints about every 18 in. along the length. I determined the approximate location of the finished end so that I could avoid the nightmare of exposing a biscuit when I made the final cut. I sand and finish counters in the shop before I scribe and install them.

When I make cabinet doors, I keep the stock as thick as possible, at least ¾ in. and ideally ⅞ in. I flatten door stock on the jointer, then run it through the thickness planer to ensure that it is flat, square-edged, and uniform thickness. Using bar clamps rather than pipe clamps can help to keep doors flat. I lay the door directly on the clamp-bar surface so that I can detect any deflection, and clamp the door to the bar using smaller clamps if necessary. I check for square by comparing diagonal measurements and hold a straightedge across the top and bottom of the frame to ensure that the rail and stile joints are glued up flat, not bowed. I also check for twist, either by sighting across the bare surface of the door or with the aid of winding sticks. Finally, I check the back of the door to make sure the panel is centered in the frame, and I adjust it if necessary by applying pressure with a wide chisel.

When the doors are dry, I rough-fit them to the cabinet openings using a handplane or a tablesaw. Then I rout and chisel mortises for the butt hinges on the cabinets' face frames; the mortises in the doors will come later.

Next, I install the case backs and the solid ledgers. These hanging strips are screwed not just through the ¼-in. plywood cabinet backs, but directly through the top, the sides, or both. If the strips go only through the back and the back should somehow detach from the case, the entire assembly can fall forward, causing damage and possibly injury.

SIZE AND WEIGHT DETERMINE HARDWARE

A drawer that's 40 in. wide requires special slides to withstand the stresses placed on it when it's fully extended. However, the full-extension, heavy-duty 12-in. drawer slides from Accuride® (model 3640; www.accuride.com) that I chose turned out to be ¼ in. longer than the inside of the base cabinets. Fortunately, cutting a hole in the cabinet's back made just enough space.

To install the drawers, we hang the drawer box first and apply the face later (see p. 19). Typically, we hang the box with special low-profile screws that can be purchased with the drawer hardware. The box should be hung initially about ⅛ in. behind its final position. In this instance, we were working with ¾-in.-thick applied drawer faces, so the box was set back ⅞ in.

ANATOMY OF A BUILT-IN

Segmented construction let us assemble everything in the shop, break it down, and reassemble it in the kitchen. After the plywood boxes were screwed together in the shop, individual solid-wood face frames were glued to each box. The center cabinets had a complete face frame, while each side cabinet's frame, when joined to the center, would share the center's left or right stile.

At the client's house, we reassembled the base cabinets, shimmed them level, and screwed them to the framing. After scribing the counter to fit, we screwed it to the base cabinets. We installed the upper cabinets in the same way as the lower.

FIRST ASSEMBLY IS DONE IN THE SHOP for a better final fit. After Jerry Nees glued the center face frame to the center cabinet, he clamped the base cabinets together in the shop. The left and right portions of the face frame then can be scribed to fit and glued to their respective cabinets. The process is repeated for the upper cabinets.

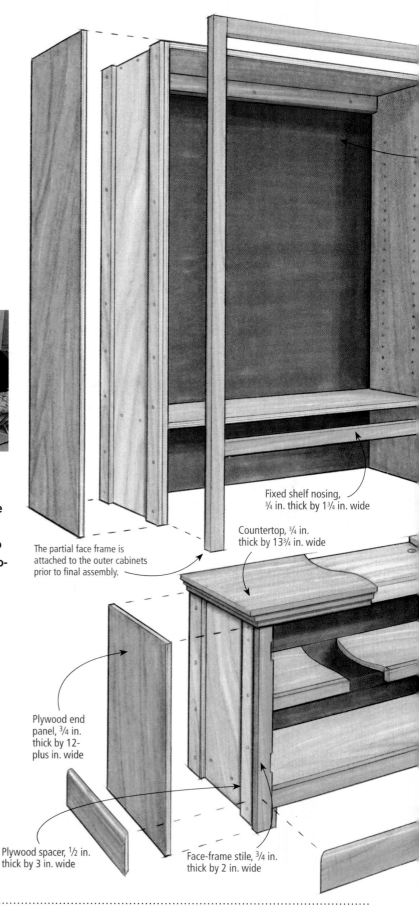

Fixed shelf nosing, ¾ in. thick by 1¾ in. wide

Countertop, ¾ in. thick by 13¾ in. wide

The partial face frame is attached to the outer cabinets prior to final assembly.

Plywood end panel, ¾ in. thick by 12-plus in. wide

Plywood spacer, ½ in. thick by 3 in. wide

Face-frame stile, ¾ in. thick by 2 in. wide

UNDERCOUNTER MOLDING DETAIL

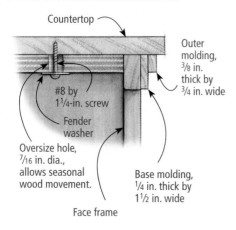

Countertop

Outer molding, ⅜ in. thick by ¾ in. wide

#8 by 1¼-in. screw

Fender washer

Oversize hole, 7/16 in. dia., allows seasonal wood movement.

Base molding, ¼ in. thick by 1½ in. wide

Face frame

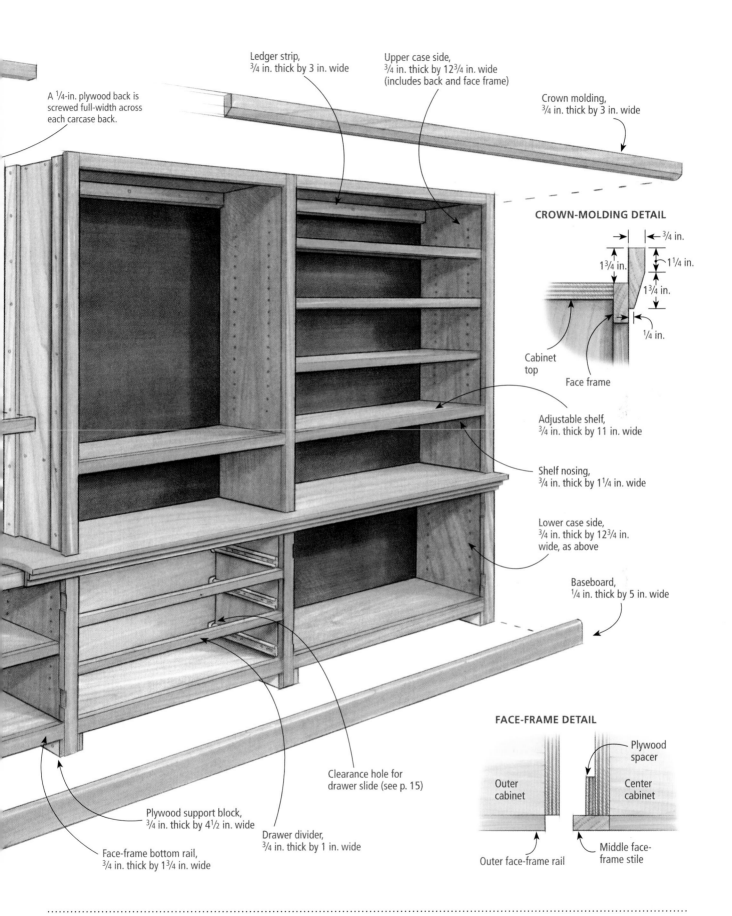

A ¼-in. plywood back is screwed full-width across each carcase back.

Ledger strip, ¾ in. thick by 3 in. wide

Upper case side, ¾ in. thick by 12¾ in. wide (includes back and face frame)

Crown molding, ¾ in. thick by 3 in. wide

CROWN-MOLDING DETAIL

¾ in.

1¾ in.

1¼ in.

1¾ in.

¼ in.

Cabinet top

Face frame

Adjustable shelf, ¾ in. thick by 11 in. wide

Shelf nosing, ¾ in. thick by 1¼ in. wide

Lower case side, ¾ in. thick by 12¾ in. wide, as above

Baseboard, ¼ in. thick by 5 in. wide

Clearance hole for drawer slide (see p. 15)

Plywood support block, ¾ in. thick by 4½ in. wide

Drawer divider, ¾ in. thick by 1 in. wide

Face-frame bottom rail, ¾ in. thick by 1¾ in. wide

FACE-FRAME DETAIL

Plywood spacer

Outer cabinet

Center cabinet

Outer face-frame rail

Middle face-frame stile

SOLID DETAILS FOR LONG-LASTING DOORS

For most cabinet doors, I make stiles and rails from stock that's slightly thicker than ³/₄ in. I prefer to use mortise-and-tenon joinery (drawing right), but cope-and-stick is also a viable option (drawing below). I cut the grooves and tenons on the tablesaw, using a dado blade and (for the tenons) a sliding miter gauge. I use a ⁵/₁₆-in.-wide mortise-and-tenon joint; I have found that my mortising machine's ⁵/₁₆-in.-dia. auger bit and hollow chisel are less likely to break from overheating than are ¹/₄-in. tools. My door panels are typically solid wood. If the groove is ¹/₂ in. deep, I make the panel ¹/₈ in. less all around to allow for some expansion. In summer, when the relative humidity is high here in Indiana, I make the panels extend closer to ⁷/₁₆ in. into a ¹/₂-in.-deep groove.

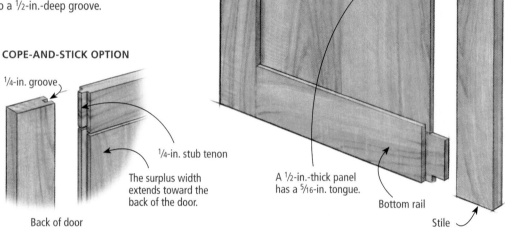

COPE-AND-STICK OPTION

¹/₄-in. groove

¹/₄-in. stub tenon

The surplus width extends toward the back of the door.

Back of door

Top rail

⁵/₁₆-in. haunch

⁵/₁₆-in. groove

⁵/₁₆-in.-wide groove

A ¹/₂-in.-thick panel has a ⁵/₁₆-in. tongue.

Bottom rail

Stile

Start at the floor's highest point

Because this design called for an applied base molding, I could shim the casework up to level and count on the baseboard to hide the shims. I began from the high point on the floor and shimmed the cases up to level as necessary. The sections also were clamped together, so I could treat the three cabinets as a single unit if the wall behind them wasn't flat.

I use solid wood for counters because it generally holds up better than plywood and looks better with wear. When a solid counter is attached to a plywood case, the wood has to be able to move with changes in relative humidity. I set the counter in place and scribe as necessary, then attach it with screws in oversize holes that allow for wood movement.

As with the bases, I scribe the right face-frame stile to conform to irregularities in the wall, then screw together the upper units to form a single assembly before attaching it to the rear wall. No shimming is necessary because these upper cases are placed on a surface that should be level. I scribe the finished ends as needed and glue them in place. I also sand the face-frame edges flush if necessary.

Hang the doors and drawers

After applying the baseboard and crown molding, we work on the doors. For inset applications, I like to plane doors and drawer faces to size after installing the casework. Although this technique is unconventional, I find it more efficient. Once in their final position, cabinets don't always sit quite the way they did in the ideal conditions of the shop, so postponing this final fitting until the installation is complete means the work is done only once.

After shimming the doors in place with the proper margins (about 3/32 in. for stain grade, more for painted work), I mark the positions of the hinge mortises on the door stiles. Once marked, the door is clamped in a vise or on sawhorses, where I rout the mortises and mount the hinges. Once the door is rehung, I do a final fitting with a handplane.

Setting the drawers is the final stage. After finalizing the fit, I use a pair of screws and fender washers to hold the drawer face in position. Once I'm satisfied with the fit, I drive in four additional screws to lock the face to the drawer box.

Nancy R. Hiller (www.nrhillerdesign.com) is a professional maker of custom furniture and cabinetry based in Bloomington, Ind. She specializes in period-authentic furniture and built-ins for homes and offices from the late-19th through mid-20th centuries. Photos by Kendall Reeves. Illustrations by Bob La Pointe.

HANG THE DRAWER BOX, THEN ATTACH THE FACE

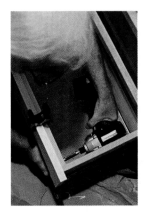

I usually make drawers from 1/2-in. solid stock and dovetail the corners; it's a joinery option that my customers expect. (For less-expensive projects, I use biscuits or a rabbeted joint, as shown in the detail drawings at right.) I groove the inside faces of the front and sides to accept the drawer bottom (I use 3/8-in.- or 1/2-in.-thick plywood for the bottoms of extrawide drawers to prevent them from sagging). I also rip the back even with the top face of the drawer bottom so that I can slide in the bottom once the drawer sides are glued. Securing the bottom with small screws (but no glue) provides the option of a removable drawer bottom.

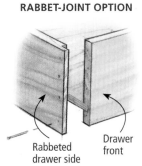

RABBET-JOINT OPTION

Rabbeted drawer side

Drawer front

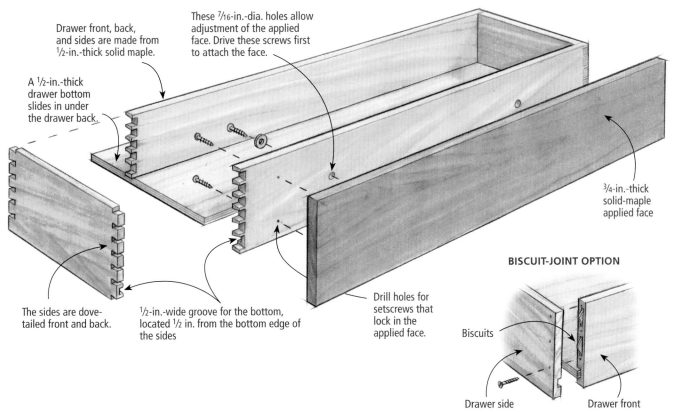

Drawer front, back, and sides are made from 1/2-in.-thick solid maple.

These 7/16-in.-dia. holes allow adjustment of the applied face. Drive these screws first to attach the face.

A 1/2-in.-thick drawer bottom slides in under the drawer back.

3/4-in.-thick solid-maple applied face

The sides are dovetailed front and back.

1/2-in.-wide groove for the bottom, located 1/2 in. from the bottom edge of the sides

Drill holes for setscrews that lock in the applied face.

BISCUIT-JOINT OPTION

Biscuits

Drawer side

Drawer front

A Space-Saving Island with Drawers

BY JOSEPH B. LANZA   I recently renovated a carriage house that was to be used for entertaining or for extended stays from my clients' family. On the upper level, more than half of the 20-ft. by 24-ft. space was

taken up by the kitchen. To make the kitchen efficient, the clients and I wanted the island to be a space for working as well as for gathering and eating.

A few issues came up as I designed the rest of the kitchen. For example, positioning the sink and the major appliances along the outside wall wouldn't leave much space for storage. To have room for seating, the island needed an overhanging counter on three sides, which left room for only two base cabinets. I knew that the big overhang would create space for drawers below the top, a detail seen on many tables. Table-style legs on an island of this size, though, would look bulky and would interfere with seating. My challenge became how to support drawers without legs. Here was my solution: Two plywood base cabinets with solid, substantial tops and backs support a frame of 5/4 poplar glued and screwed together and skinned with a piece of ½-in. birch plywood. This frame supports a countertop of solid 6/4 maple, which, in turn, stiffens and supports the frame. The frame carries the drawers on side-mount slides to save space. The base is covered with 4/4 walnut random-width beadboard, drawers, and door fronts.

Start with the boxes

I'm a big fan of simple cabinet boxes, and these boxes fit that category perfectly. I often use ¾-in. birch plywood, and I glue, nail, and screw the butt joints together. I wanted these two cabinets to be able to support the big maple top, so I stiffened them with ¾-in. backs and full (rather than strip) tops. One cabinet holds the microwave, and the other features a drawer above a pair of doors.

At the site, I marked the locations for the boxes and screwed 2x cleats to the floor just inside their footprints at each end. Between where the two cabinets would rest, I anchored another cleat the same thickness as the frame and screwed the cabinets to the cleats.

Integrate the frame with the boxes

To support the top and to house the drawers, I made a frame of 5/4x5 poplar that would extend beyond the cabinets approximately 14 in. To make a more positive connection with the plywood subtop, I cut a ½-in.-deep

rabbet along the edge of both end pieces and ripped the remaining pieces down to 4½ in. I cut bridle joints at the appropriate points and attached the frame with glue and screws. I cut the plywood to size, and screwed and glued it to the top of the frame.

Final assembly

Back at the site, I installed the face frames and attached the beadboard. After installing the drawers and their Blum undermount slides on the work side, I hung the doors and the drawer fronts. On the seating side of the island, I installed the drawers with Accuride-style side-mount slides. I completed the job by finishing both the walnut base and the maple top with three coats of Ceramithane, a waterborne urethane.

Joseph Lanza (www.josephlanza.com) designs and builds entire houses, as well as their parts, in Duxbury, Mass. Illustrations by John Hartman.

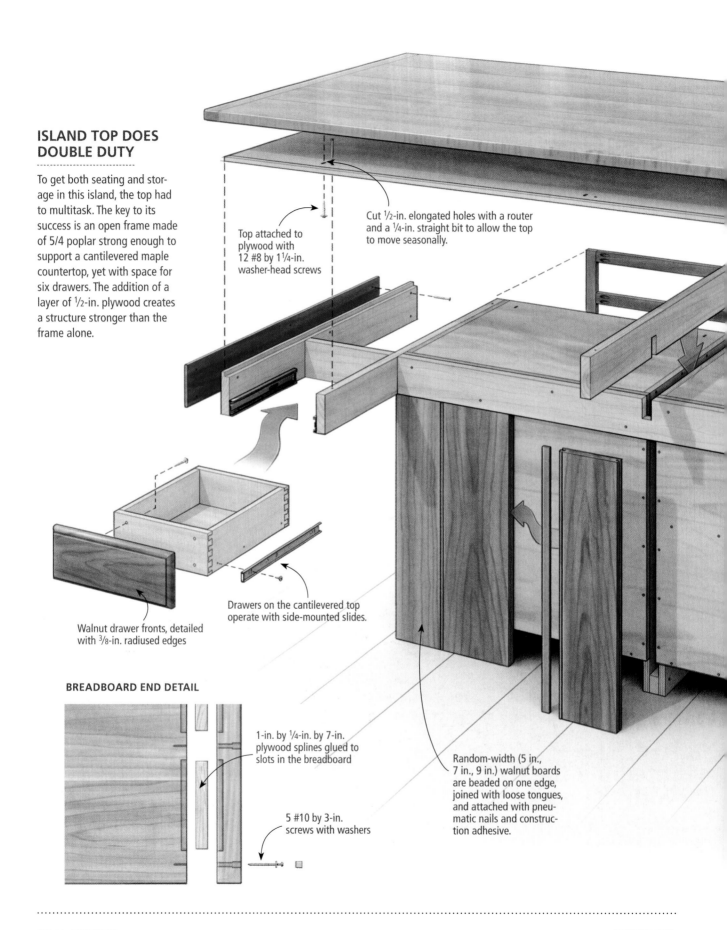

ISLAND TOP DOES DOUBLE DUTY

To get both seating and storage in this island, the top had to multitask. The key to its success is an open frame made of 5/4 poplar strong enough to support a cantilevered maple countertop, yet with space for six drawers. The addition of a layer of ½-in. plywood creates a structure stronger than the frame alone.

Top attached to plywood with 12 #8 by 1¼-in. washer-head screws

Cut ½-in. elongated holes with a router and a ¼-in. straight bit to allow the top to move seasonally.

Drawers on the cantilevered top operate with side-mounted slides.

Walnut drawer fronts, detailed with ³⁄₈-in. radiused edges

BREADBOARD END DETAIL

1-in. by ¼-in. by 7-in. plywood splines glued to slots in the breadboard

5 #10 by 3-in. screws with washers

Random-width (5 in., 7 in., 9 in.) walnut boards are beaded on one edge, joined with loose tongues, and attached with pneumatic nails and construction adhesive.

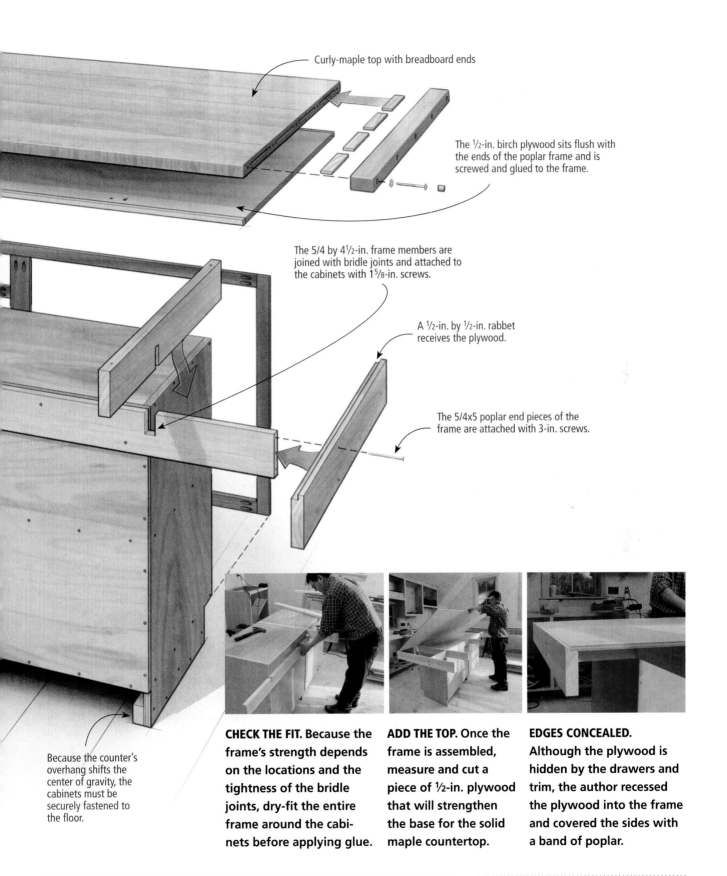

Curly-maple top with breadboard ends

The ½-in. birch plywood sits flush with the ends of the poplar frame and is screwed and glued to the frame.

The 5/4 by 4½-in. frame members are joined with bridle joints and attached to the cabinets with 1⅝-in. screws.

A ½-in. by ½-in. rabbet receives the plywood.

The 5/4x5 poplar end pieces of the frame are attached with 3-in. screws.

Because the counter's overhang shifts the center of gravity, the cabinets must be securely fastened to the floor.

CHECK THE FIT. Because the frame's strength depends on the locations and the tightness of the bridle joints, dry-fit the entire frame around the cabinets before applying glue.

ADD THE TOP. Once the frame is assembled, measure and cut a piece of ½-in. plywood that will strengthen the base for the solid maple countertop.

EDGES CONCEALED. Although the plywood is hidden by the drawers and trim, the author recessed the plywood into the frame and covered the sides with a band of poplar.

Design the Perfect Pantry

BY PAUL DEGROOT ■ Ask your neighbors what they dislike about their pantries, and you'll likely get an earful: "It's too small" or "I can't find anything in it." I hear these complaints on cue from clients. Clearly, the way we store our soup and cereal warrants careful planning.

Whether you are building a new kitchen or remodeling what you have, you need to consider what makes a pantry work and which kind is best for your situation. Here, I'll describe the three main types of pantries: cabinets, reach-ins, and walk-ins. I'll also offer a suggestion for a hybrid pantry/mudroom that the homeowners walk through as they enter the house. The drawings are meant to illustrate the basics; the photos show some of my actual projects.

Just keep two things in mind as you read and plan your pantry: Good design means keeping things simple, and the

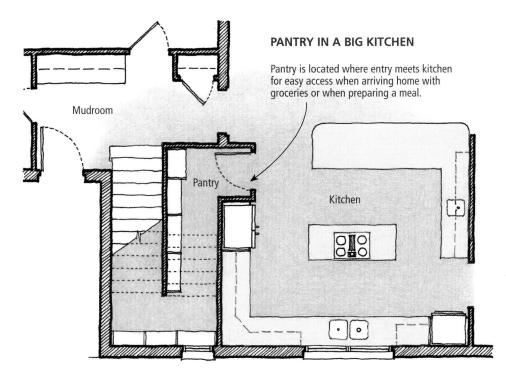

Pantry is located where entry meets kitchen for easy access when arriving home with groceries or when preparing a meal.

Mudroom

Pantry

Kitchen

LOCATION, LOCATION, LOCATION

An efficient smaller kitchen has the pantry on one side of the stove, separated by about 4 ft. of counter, and the refrigerator on the other side of the stove, separated by a similar stretch of counter. Both sides of the stove are convenient prep zones. In larger kitchens, the pantry also should be near a working counter or an island and preferably near the doorway where groceries enter the home.

right location often trumps size. Sometimes, a hardworking cabinet is all you need for convenient access to all your kitchen goods.

The basics: location and lighting

Convenience and visibility are the essential attributes of a great pantry. Regardless of size, the pantry should be in a handy location, positioned in the kitchen or immediately next to it. A modest pantry cabinet placed within the kitchen footprint will be more convenient for regular use than an oversize walk-in down the hall. Plus, every pantry's utility will be improved with counter space for sorting and unloading groceries.

Pantries also must have proper lighting so that you can see the contents well. Ceiling-mounted linear fluorescents work well for walk-in pantries. Install the fixtures parallel to the longest shelving runs for best light. Due to the extra cost, most of the cabinet pantries I design don't have internal lighting, so I make sure that there is ade-

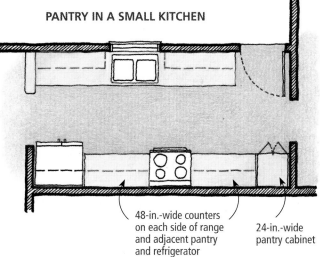

PANTRY IN A SMALL KITCHEN

48-in.-wide counters on each side of range and adjacent pantry and refrigerator

24-in.-wide pantry cabinet

quate kitchen lighting directly outside the cabinet. Often, this means that I will locate one or two recessed fixtures about 16 in. from the face of the cabinet. A reach-in closet pantry will benefit from a low-profile fluorescent light mounted inside, especially when a tall header blocks ambient light from the high shelves. I specify slim, no-frills fluorescents with rounded acrylic diffusers for these above-door applications.

CABINET PANTRY

This type of pantry requires the smallest footprint, but it can still pack a lot of storage. Cabinet pantries can be stock items ordered from national cabinet shops, or they can be custom-built from designers' plans. The author prefers the arrangement shown here: a full-height, cabinet-depth pantry with fully extending drawers below a series of pullouts and stationary shelves. Depending on the width of the pantry, it may have a single door or a pair of doors no wider than 18 in. each.

LIGHT YOU DON'T HAVE TO THINK ABOUT. Good lighting allows you to see clearly. A fixture should be placed inside the pantry or on the ceiling directly outside it. A door-operated switch means you don't have to turn the light on manually or remember to turn it off.

BLOCKING FOR CLEARANCE. The drawback of sliding shelves behind doors is that the inside of the doors tends to get scratched. The farther you can fur out the shelves from the inside of the cabinet, the better the chance of keeping the doors in good shape.

PLAN VIEW

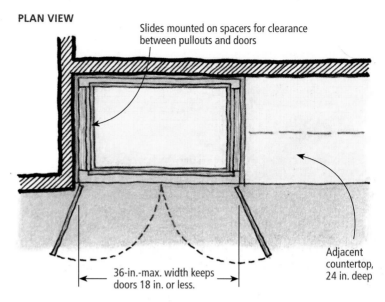

Slides mounted on spacers for clearance between pullouts and doors

Adjacent countertop, 24 in. deep

36-in.-max. width keeps doors 18 in. or less.

ELEVATION

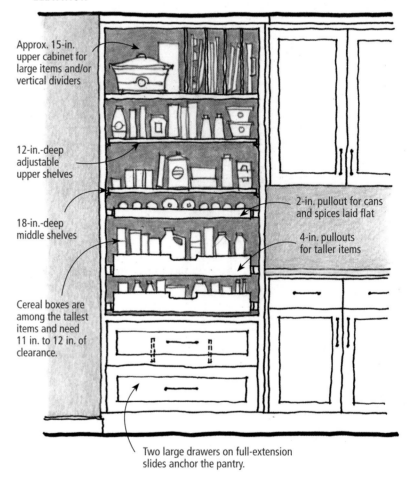

Approx. 15-in. upper cabinet for large items and/or vertical dividers

12-in.-deep adjustable upper shelves

18-in.-deep middle shelves

Cereal boxes are among the tallest items and need 11 in. to 12 in. of clearance.

2-in. pullout for cans and spices laid flat

4-in. pullouts for taller items

Two large drawers on full-extension slides anchor the pantry.

Electrical codes are strict about the types and the locations of lights installed in closets. Treat pantry lighting with similar caution. If you must use incandescent fixtures, be sure to place them well away from any open shelves that might be packed with paper goods and combustibles.

A better pantry may not be bigger

Cabinet pantries are space efficient, typically occupying just 4 sq. ft. to 8 sq. ft. of floor area. For big families and others who buy in bulk, I sometimes supplement the in-kitchen pantry cabinet with a larger pantry elsewhere.

Reach-in closet pantries range in size from 6 sq. ft. to 12 sq. ft., assuming a 24-in. depth and a width from 3 ft. to 6 ft. There are occasions where a 24-in. depth is not possible. In these cases, a 12-in. depth is the minimum, but 16 in. or more would allow some storage flexibility. It's difficult to see and access items at the extreme sides of a wide reach-in closet pantry with a narrow doorway. Except on the smallest of reach-ins, I use pairs of doors with the sidewalls of the closet no more than 6 in. from each door jamb.

Surrounded by 2x4 stud walls, pantry closets waste a fair amount of volume with studs and drywall. A simple remodeling strategy is to substitute a tall cabinet pantry in the same location as an old closet. Trading a 4½-in.-thick wall for a ¾-in. plywood end panel nets inches of extra shelf width. The result is a user-friendly pantry in a compact package that can match the rest of the kitchen cabinets.

A compact walk-in can be made with an interior footprint of about 4 ft. by 4 ft. and an L-shaped arrangement of shelves on two walls. While the length of the room is variable, the width depends on the shelving arrangement and the walking aisle. I consider 44 in. to be a minimum width, affording a 28-in. aisle and 16-in. shelves on one wall only. A long, narrow room like this will still feel tight. Widening such a pantry allows for more comfortable browsing space, wider shelves, and/or shelves on two parallel walls. Note that a room wider than 8 ft. will likely have wasted floor space in the middle. A typical walk-in pantry might take up 30 sq. ft., at 6 ft. wide by 5 ft. deep. A large walk-in could easily double that area, especially if a client wants room for a counter, a step stool, and a spare refrigerator.

HARDWORKING DOORS. Using the back side of a cabinet-pantry door for storage takes away from the potential depth of shelves, but it offers an area where commonly used goods won't get lost in the clutter.

It's all about storage

While deep shelves can hold more stuff, it's a frustrated cook who can't find the rice hidden behind a train wreck of juice boxes and pasta. For better visibility, I like to stagger the depth of shelves.

A simple pantry with fixed wooden shelving is quick and easy to build. If your budget dictates this approach,

CONT'D ON PAGE 30 ▶

REACH-IN PANTRY

Enclosed by stud walls, this pantry is a small closet. Reach-in closet pantries tend to be affordable and easy to build. Some have pairs of doors concealing 4 ft. to 7 ft. of shelving across the back wall. Better reach-ins have the widest doors possible for good visibility of the contents. Considering that wide doors take up substantial wall space, this pantry is best located just off the kitchen proper so that the kitchen walls can be loaded with cabinets, appliances, windows, and other essentials.

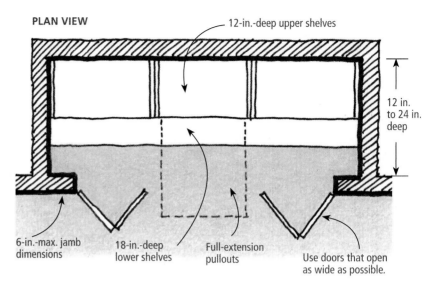

PLAN VIEW

12-in.-deep upper shelves

12 in. to 24 in. deep

6-in.-max. jamb dimensions

18-in.-deep lower shelves

Full-extension pullouts

Use doors that open as wide as possible.

REACH IN, ONCE IN A WHILE. Commonly used goods are stored in the cabinet pantry seen inside the kitchen. Nearby, a secondary reach-in pantry holds the bulk and is used for restocking.

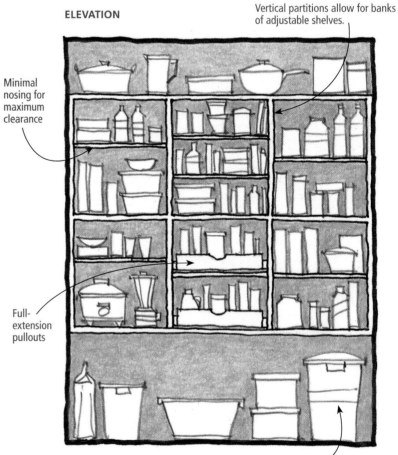

ELEVATION

Vertical partitions allow for banks of adjustable shelves.

Minimal nosing for maximum clearance

Full-extension pullouts

A 24-in.-tall bottom shelf leaves room on the floor to store tall items.

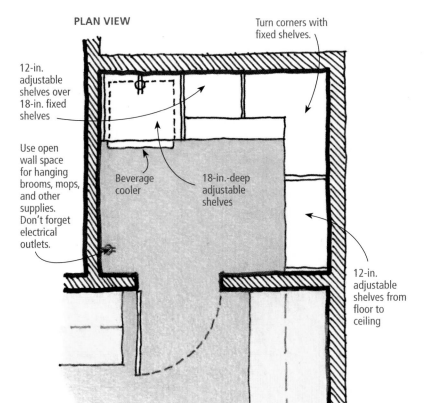

PLAN VIEW

Turn corners with fixed shelves.

12-in. adjustable shelves over 18-in. fixed shelves

Use open wall space for hanging brooms, mops, and other supplies. Don't forget electrical outlets.

Beverage cooler

18-in.-deep adjustable shelves

12-in. adjustable shelves from floor to ceiling

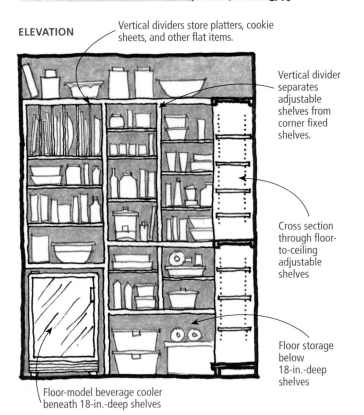

ELEVATION

Vertical dividers store platters, cookie sheets, and other flat items.

Vertical divider separates adjustable shelves from corner fixed shelves.

Cross section through floor-to-ceiling adjustable shelves

Floor storage below 18-in.-deep shelves

Floor-model beverage cooler beneath 18-in.-deep shelves

WALK-IN PANTRY

Usually the biggest of the lot, a walk-in pantry is ideal for those who buy in bulk and/or live far from the grocery store. Roomy walk-ins are large enough to use three or four walls for storing items such as dry goods, paper towels, pet food, appliances, and brooms. Smaller walk-ins usually have just two walls of shelving. A popular and affordable option for a small walk-in pantry is to put it in a corner of the kitchen, with the door set on a 45° angle between adjoining counters. For those wanting fewer cabinets and an open, minimalistic look in their kitchen, a walk-in pantry just outside the room can be a solution that doesn't compromise the kitchen aesthetic.

WALK IN TO CONVENIENCE. For a family that buys in bulk, a large walk-in pantry not only hides groceries, but it also offers a place for a second fridge and freezer as well as a beverage cooler.

consider mounting 16-in.-deep to 18-in.-deep shelves starting about 24 in. above the floor so that you can keep taller items on the floor below. At eye level, switch to 12-in.-deep shelves. Bulkier items on the lower shelves may be taller than 12 in., a common vertical shelf spacing, so allow extra height there—if not all the way across a wall then at least across a portion of it. However, it is common to experience a trial-and-error fitting when first loading a new pantry, so adjustable shelves rate highly on the convenience meter. They also readily accommodate an additional shelf.

For full-height cabinet pantries, I position two big full-extension drawers nearest the floor, enabling items stored in the back to be found easily. Above these drawers, I usually spec a pair of tall doors concealing a combination of pullouts and fixed shelves. This way, users can see the entire pantry at once. I sometimes add a second pair of shorter doors at the top of the cabinet. This space is good for oversize items that are used infrequently. It also can be outfitted with vertical dividers for cookie sheets and the like.

User preferences and heights dictate modifications to my basic cabinet-pantry template. Tall folks may want an additional pullout inside the main compartment. Some like spice racks or small shelves mounted on the inside of the cabinet doors.

Narrow spaces in a base-cabinet arrangement also can be used for pullout pantry units, where the entire assembly extends out from the cabinet frame. Either custom-built or ordered from a catalog, these units have front panels hiding multiple shelves behind, with access gained from both sides when the units slide out. Häfele®, Rev-A-Shelf®, and others sell cabinet-pantry hardware narrow enough to squeeze into a 4-in.-wide space.

Don't forget that wall space inside a walk-in pantry is useful for hanging a mop and brooms, so don't put shelves everywhere.

Give some thought to keeping small appliances in the pantry, plugged in and ready to use. A deep pantry shelf or counter is a possible location for a seldom-used microwave oven. I have a client who keeps a toaster and coffeemaker in her walk-in pantry to reduce the clutter on her counters. Built-in beverage centers take up valuable kitchen real estate. I saved money by putting a freestanding model in our pantry below the staircase.

Doors shouldn't get in the way

While I almost always use standard 24-in.-deep units for cabinet pantries, the width depends on the design specifics of the kitchen. Maintaining a width of 36 in. or less allows me a pair of cabinet doors, each less than 18 in. across. Wider doors can be heavy and unwieldy to open. When I have more than 36 in. of width for a built-in pantry, I place two separate cabinets side-by-side, with three or four doors across the front.

Have you ever had a closet with cheap bifold doors? Used daily, the light-duty hardware gives out; the doors stop gliding and eventually derail. It doesn't have to be so. Outfitted with commercial-grade hardware, bifold door panels are good options for wider reach-in pantry closets. The beauty of these doors is their ability to provide wide openings while being unobtrusive when open. I like to use a pocket door when it is likely to remain open quite a bit or when a swinging door is going to be in the way.

WALK-THROUGH PANTRY

Sometimes the pantry is part of a mudroom or utility room next to the kitchen. It's often a walk-through room instead of a walk-in. A good example is a pantry/mudroom you pass through from the garage or back porch to the kitchen. This arrangement provides a handy place to wipe your feet and put away items. Storage can be out of view behind doors, or it can be open shelving and bins lining the walls. As a mudroom, it needs space for stowing backpacks, feeding the dog, charging a smart phone, or washing dirty hands. Some might allocate space for an extra freezer or refrigerator.

PUT IT AWAY ON THE WAY IN. A hybrid pantry/mudroom located between the garage and the kitchen is convenient when you arrive home with groceries and when you are preparing dinner. Counter space near the pantry is always a good idea.

PLAN VIEW

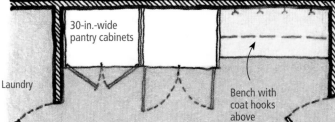

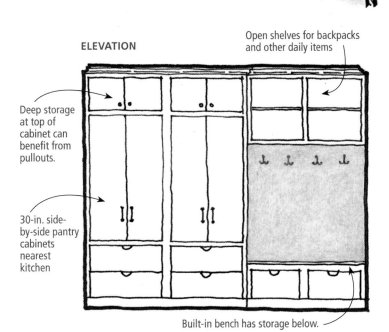

For a single door to a walk-in pantry, I never use less than a 24 in. width, but most folks will appreciate the extra passage of a 30-in. door. You will need a 32-in.-wide door if a big appliance has to get through it, but don't forget that swinging doors take up space. A wide pantry door that opens against a counter will block access. With outswing pantry doors, I keep the doorknob nearest the counter for best functionality. When an outswinger won't work, I fit a pocket door into the blueprint or arrange an inswinger to park against an unused interior wall.

Finally, an automatic light switch that is activated by the door is a nice touch for a pantry because you're likely to be coming or going with your hands full.

Paul DeGroot (www.degrootarchitect.com) is an architect who designs custom homes and additions in Austin, Texas. Drawings by the author. Photo p. 30 by Samuel Pontolilo.

Taming an Outdated Pantry

BY JOSEPH LANZA ▪ When we first started remodeling our house, space and time were tight. After I carved out a small office behind the kitchen, I was left with a space about 5½ ft. by 7½ ft. to serve as the laundry, the pantry, and a broom closet. We put a stacked washer/dryer in the corner by the kitchen door. On the wall next to it, I hung some heavy-duty wire shelving above the litter box. On the opposite wall, I built some plywood shelves to hold cans and boxes of food. This system worked while we readied an addition.

When the addition was complete, the laundry moved out, and more recycling boxes and wire shelving moved in. We knew we could do a lot more with the space. After eight or nine years of thinking about it, we had a pretty good idea of what we wanted, so I started modeling the pantry in SketchUp. An additional sink to handle houseplants and cleaning was first on the wish list. Recycling was next. I've built or installed a few kitchen-cabinet recycling centers, but they all have required transferring recyclables to another container on the way to the street. I liked the simplicity of tossing the stuff right into the curbside container. I didn't see why it wouldn't work inside a cabinet, preferably under the sink.

I brought the wall cabinets right up to the sloped ceiling. I knew this wouldn't get us much more usable

CABINETS DON'T MAKE THE SPACE BIGGER, but they do add efficiency and appeal. Formerly a cramped storage space (photo, facing page), the pantry was transformed into a good-looking room with lots more storage by the addition of well-designed, simple, and elegant cabinets.

SQUEEZING THE MOST FROM 40 SQ. FT.

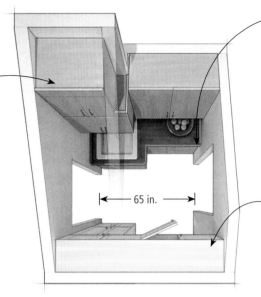

NEW UPPER CABINETS

Instead of the usual 12-in.-deep uppers, the author made the new cabinets 16 in. deep. They can store a lot of stuff (serving bowls, lunch boxes, coolers, big wine bottles laid on their sides) that would never fit in a standard wall cabinet, as well as dishes and glassware.

65 in.

NEW BASE CABINETS

The finished-maple plywood cabinet boxes were assembled with butt joints, glue, and screws. The width of the sink base, 30½ in., was limited by the swing of the exterior door. To make sure that the recycling bin would fit underneath, the author made the base cabinets 27 in. deep and pushed the sink slightly off center. Now that the bin had a place, he could use the other 32-in.-wide base cabinet for drawers, which offer much more efficient storage than shelves.

DOORS FOR EXISTING SHELVES

The paint-grade cabinets use the wall space between the kitchen and office doors, including the space over the office door. They contain adjustable shelves used to store canned and dry goods, and at 12 in. deep, they don't interfere with traffic flow.

space and also would make building the cabinets a bit more complicated, but it would get me out of building a soffit.

A scrap of plywood becomes a layout tool

After figuring out the basic design in SketchUp, I worked out the final dimensions at full scale using a story stick that I made from a scrap piece of plywood about 2 in. wide, cut to fit exactly between the walls of the spaces. Starting with the base cabinets, I held the stick in place and marked the edge of the plumbing pipes running on the outside of the left-hand wall, then opened the back door to see how much room I had for the sink base. I added a couple of inches beyond the swing of the door for the end panel and the countertop overhang, then marked out the cabinet between those marks on the stick. For the upper cabinets, I turned the same story stick over and held it against the back wall. I marked the corner where the wall jogs, then laid out the cabinets to the left and right. I drew all the components—cabinet sides, spacers, blocks, and scribe strips—on the story stick, then used the story stick (instead of my tape measure) to mark the plywood when I cut out the cabinet parts.

CHECK YOUR WORK. A handy layout and construction tool to use on jobs like this project, a story stick is a length of plywood scrap on which room measurements are recorded and cabinet spacing is determined. Once the cabinets are installed, use the stick to double-check their locations.

ASSEMBLE THE FACE FRAMES AHEAD OF TIME. Built in the shop with pocket screws, the frames are scribed to the wall and nailed to the boxes as units.

UPPER CABINETS

Maple face frames

Baltic-birch plywood panels

Cabinet boxes are screwed through cleats into the wall framing.

During installation, cabinets are separated by plywood spacers that make room for finished end panels.

Baltic-birch plywood end panels

Build and hang the uppers first

I bought finished maple plywood for the cabinet boxes. It's pricey, but it also saves lots of time that would be spent applying finish. I built the uppers first because it was easier to install them without climbing over the base cabinets. The cabinet carcases are simple four-piece boxes (no backs) with the sides angled to follow the ceiling. I used a plunge router and a shopmade jig to drill holes for adjustable shelving, then assembled the boxes. Instead of plywood backs, I attached a poplar cleat at the back to attach the box to the wall and let the face frame square up the box. The lack of a back doesn't weaken the box, makes construction and installation easier, and in the case of the base cabinets, makes the integration of plumbing and other obstacles simpler.

I find it much easier to apply finished end panels after installation than to make the cabinets with finished sides, so during installation, I used ¾-in. spacers between the cabinets. I made the face frames from ¾-in. maple, joined with pocket screws. After hanging the boxes, I attached the face frames with glue and nails.

Next, install the kick base

I've found that it's less of a headache to build a plinth or kick base for cabinets, especially in an older house. Once the kick faces are shimmed level and attached to the floor,

I can cover them with a clean piece of finished plywood that hides the shims and screwheads.

After building the boxes, I nailed them to the bases and screwed them to the walls. When all the cabinets were installed, I applied a shellac-based sanding sealer for color and finished with two coats of water-based polyurethane.

Drawers and doors complete the project

Rather than make frame-and-panel doors and drawers, I made the doors and drawers from ¾-in. Baltic-birch ply-

BASE CABINETS

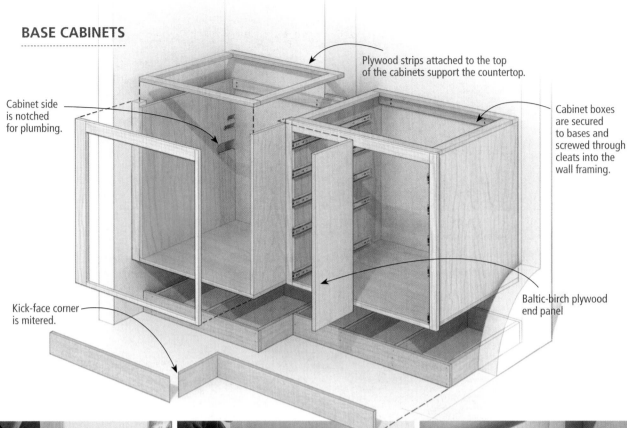

Plywood strips attached to the top of the cabinets support the countertop.

Cabinet side is notched for plumbing.

Cabinet boxes are secured to bases and screwed through cleats into the wall framing.

Kick-face corner is mitered.

Baltic-birch plywood end panel

A SEPARATE BASE IS EASY TO LEVEL. In older houses, it's often easier to build and install separate bases for the lower cabinets. Basically plywood boxes, the bases are shimmed level and attached to the floor.

A GREAT REASON FOR BACKLESS CABINETS. A backless cabinet can be placed and easily scribed to any protruding plumbing or wiring. The base cabinets are sized to create a traditional 3-in.-deep kick space below. Once the cabinets are attached to the base, the face frames are applied.

SYSTEMATIC APPROACH TO DRAWER SLIDES. Allow ¼-in. clearance between drawer fronts. Mark drawer-bottom locations on the inside cabinet wall, then transfer these marks to a piece of plywood. Use this piece inside the cabinet to support the top drawer slides while they're being attached to the cabinet sides. In turn, cut it down to the next drawer-slide height for each drawer. For the bottom drawer, rest the slide on a scrap of ¼-in. plywood on the bottom of the cabinet.

wood. It's less expensive, and I like the minimalist look. After slightly rounding over the edges and finishing them, I hung the doors with clip-on full-overlay hinges. I drilled the 35-mm holes with a drill press equipped with a fence.

For the drawers, I used side-mounted ball-bearing slides. To simplify layout and to speed up installation, I like to align the bottom of the drawer box with the bottom of the drawer slide when it is mounted on the cabinet. Once I had laid out the drawer heights on the inside of the cabinet, I used a piece of plywood cut the proper height to support each slide as it was installed.

Paint-grade cabinets began as basic shelves

I had originally built a 24-in.-wide by 80-in.-high shelving unit out of ¾-in. lauan. The top extended over the door to the opposite wall, supported in the back by the head casing and on the wall by a small cleat. It had a nailed-on poplar face frame and a few pine shelves supported with pins. To make the shelves easily adjustable (and to avoid having to paint the inside of the cabinets), I made new faces for the sides from ¼-in. finished maple, drilling holes for adjustable shelves, then gluing and nailing them over the existing cabinet sides. I also covered the shelves with the same ¼-in. plywood.

DETAILS DON'T HAVE TO COST A LOT. Instead of creating a seam between the laminate and counter's edge, attach the edging first, then apply the laminate, letting it run over the edge. After the adhesive dries, bevel both laminate and edging with one router pass.

EVEN PLYWOOD CAN LOOK GOOD. The exposed laminations of the Baltic-birch plywood used for the doors and drawer fronts become a minimal design element.

I hadn't considered doors before, but now that the other side of the pantry was closed in, open shelves didn't look right.

For the doors, I made poplar frames with ½-in. medium-density fiberboard (MDF) beadboard panels. Painted white, the cabinets combine with the new clear-finished cabinets to become an extension of the Baltic-birch and painted-beadboard cabinets in the kitchen.

Joseph Lanza (www.josephlanza.com) designs and builds entire houses, as well as their parts, in Duxbury, Mass. Illustrations by John Hartman.

NEW DOORS DRESS UP OLD SHELVES

....

Bare shelving (far left) needed more than face frames. Rather than use clear-finished doors, the author milled cope-and-stick frames, then used ½-in. MDF beadboard for the panels.

Poplar frames are ¾ in. by 2½ in. with a cope-and-stick profile.

½-in. MDF beadboard panel, rabbeted ¼ in. by ⅜ in. to fit frame profile

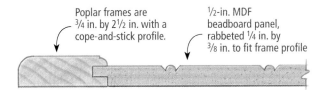

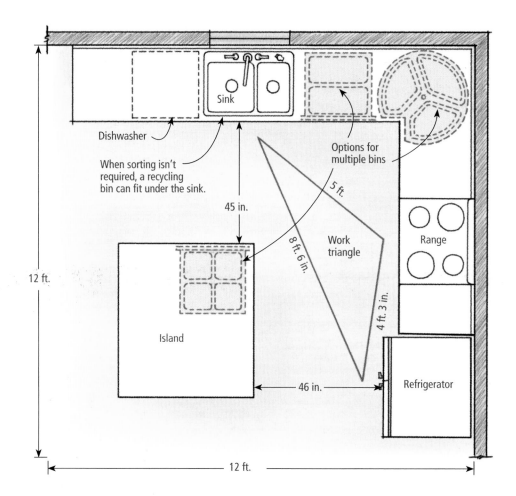

Dishwasher

When sorting isn't required, a recycling bin can fit under the sink.

Sink

Options for multiple bins

45 in.

12 ft.

5 ft.

8 ft. 6 in.

Work triangle

Range

4 ft. 3 in.

Island

46 in.

Refrigerator

12 ft.

Designing a Recycling Center

BY JAMIE GOLD   In the United States, the recycling rate for aluminum cans has hovered around 50% for years. Cans that don't make it into the recycling stream add up: Every three months, it's enough aluminum to rebuild our entire commercial air fleet.

EFFICIENT RECYCLING STORAGE IS IN THE WORK TRIANGLE

A kitchen recycling center should be within the work triangle and as close to the sink as possible. A little refresher: The three points of the triangle are the refrigerator, the sink, and the range. Traditionally, these storage, prep, and cooking areas have been arranged in a triangle to limit the travel distance between tasks. No leg should be shorter than 4 ft. or longer than 9 ft.; the sum of the legs of the triangle should be between 12 ft. and 26 ft.

Because recyclables generally need to be rinsed, keeping recycling bins near the sink eliminates extra steps. Look here first.

If you can't convert a cabinet to the immediate left or right of the sink, look along the legs of the triangle adjacent to the sink. Inside-corner cabinets are a good option for a recycling center because they typically make awkard storage for pots and pans. Lazy-susan-style holders are available with three or four bins, or you can build a custom pullout recycling station.

Perhaps the recycling rate has plateaued because people find separating and storing recyclable items inconvenient. It doesn't have to be that way. With planning and some readily available cabinet accessories, recycling can be as easy as throwing out the garbage.

Rethink storage priorities

For all the talk of the kitchen serving as the new family room, first and foremost the kitchen is where we store food, dishes, and utensils; prepare and cook meals; and clean up the mess when we're done. As shown on the facing page, these three core functions take place in the work triangle. A recycling station should be included in the work triangle because it's part of the cleanup routine.

For most homeowners, the biggest challenge in creating a recycling station is finding a place to put all those bulky containers between pickup days.

If you are worried about devoting valuable cabinet space to cast-off containers, rethink your storage allocations. Free space in the work triangle by moving infrequently used items to more-distant storage.

Recycling basics

Consider several things when you're planning a recycling station. First, how frequently are recyclable items picked up or driven to the transfer station? How many recyclables do you generate between pickups?

Next, does your municipality require that you sort recyclables? Do you have to put them at the curb in regulation containers? The answers to these questions shape the flow of cans, bottles, plastic containers, and other recyclables through your house.

To meet the bare-minimum disposal needs of a household with weekly pickups of trash and recyclables, you need two 27-quart trash bins: one for garbage, the second for recyclable items. Households with kids and/or pets need larger bins. The two-bin scenario assumes you're not required to sort recyclables. If you have to sort, you probably need four bins (metal, plastic, glass, and garbage). Even if you separate materials, I suggest avoiding bins smaller than 27 quarts because they fill too quickly. Paper

A CART ADDS A RECYCLING CENTER TO A SMALL KITCHEN

Cabinet space is usually at a premium in a small kitchen, so giving up a 15-in.-wide cabinet to store empty bottles and containers might be a tough pill to swallow. In kitchens this small, counter space is also at a premium; you might be able to kill two birds with one work cart. The cart provides workspace on the top, slide-out recycling bins at waist height, and a storage shelf below. The cart can be wheeled into the work triangle when needed.

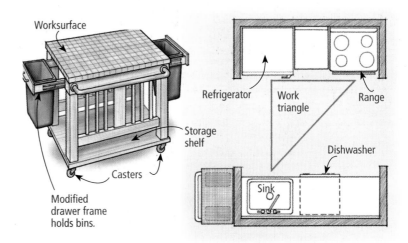

Worksurface

Storage shelf

Casters

Modified drawer frame holds bins.

Refrigerator

Work triangle

Range

Dishwasher

Sink

recycling shouldn't be included in a kitchen work triangle. I recommend an attractive basket under a family-room end table or in a home-office area where newspapers and magazines are usually read.

I try to locate a kitchen recycling center close to the sink. This placement makes rinsing out containers and disposing of them seamless. The two most-logical choices are an undersink cabinet or a cabinet to the side of the sink. For a double-bin pullout, you need a minimum 15-in. base cabinet. A four-bin pullout requires at least a 24-in. opening (a 27-in. base cabinet).

If you're setting up a recycling station in an existing kitchen where the cabinets adjacent to the sink aren't available, try taking over some base cabinets that are too small for storing pots and pans easily.

Corner cabinets are awkward for utensil and appliance storage, but they can be converted to efficient recycling storage. One off-the-shelf option is a lazy-susan-type rack that holds three bins ("Sources," at right).

Making recycling work in a small kitchen

If your kitchen is so small that you can't devote a 15-in. cabinet to a pair of recycling bins, you probably wish you had more counter space as well. A mobile prep cart could be a solution to both of these problems. As shown in the drawing on p. 39, modified drawer frames on each end of the cart can hold bins for recyclables or garbage. Your challenge will be finding floor space to park the cart.

When recycling storage must be outside the kitchen, consider the path recyclable materials take through the

SOURCES

If you're looking for hardware and other products that can help create a recycling center, these sources are a good place to start.

- www.richelieu.com
- www.knapeandvogt.com
- www.amerock.com
- www.rev-a-shelf.com
- www.hafele.com
- www.petermeier.com

house. Because recyclables typically move from the kitchen to the car or the curb for transit to the local recycling center, a point of storage convenient to your garage could be the next-best option. This location could be the garage itself, a mudroom, or a laundry area. Many homes have extra sinks in these spaces, providing a convenient place to rinse recyclables before storage and pickup.

In these locations, you can use a trash bin, your community-issued curbside container, or a repurposed container.

A laundry room adjacent to the kitchen and garage is ideal because it has a water supply. In a mudroom, the interior of a flip-up bench can be divided to hold recycling containers and still match the existing cabinetry in the room.

Jamie Gold, CKD, CAPS, is a Certified Kitchen Designer in San Diego and the author of *New Kitchen Ideas That Work* (The Taunton Press, 2012). You can find her designs and blog online at www.jgkitchens.com. Illustrations by Chuck Lockhart.

RECYCLING OUTSIDE THE KITCHEN

When you can't find space in the work triangle for a recycling center, look at the route that recyclable materials take through the house. For many people, kitchen bins are a way station before recyclables are moved to the curb. If your curbside bins are kept in the garage, you might find room in a mudroom between the kitchen and the garage. One solution that I've used with success is a bench with bins under a hinged lid. The same bench design also works on a back porch off the kitchen.

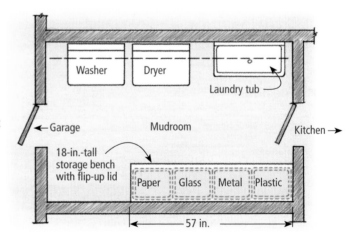

Washer | Dryer | Laundry tub

← Garage   Mudroom   Kitchen →

18-in.-tall storage bench with flip-up lid

Paper | Glass | Metal | Plastic

←— 57 in. —→

Upgrade to a Trash Drawer

BY REX ALEXANDER ■ After I've built and installed a custom kitchen, the feature that gets the most praise isn't the finish, the way I've carefully aligned the grain patterns, or the consistent reveals around the doors and drawers. It's always the pullout trash drawer, and for good reason. Not only

does the trash drawer hide refuse and recyclables, but it also helps to contain the odor that can come from an empty cat-food can or the grease from last night's dinner.

The best aspect of this design is that it can be an easy upgrade to integrate a drawer into an existing cabinet, preferably in or near the sink base. Once you've built the drawer, it's only a matter of removing the cabinet door and installing new drawer slides. Commercially produced versions are available, but why spend the money when you can do it yourself for a few bucks?

The materials are easy to find in any home center or lumberyard. I've found that a good size for the plastic wastebasket is about 10 in. wide, 14 in. deep, and 16 in. tall, which leaves enough room for a drawer above. For drawer slides, I use simple epoxy-coated, side-mount models from Blum® (www.blum.com). They are inexpensive, but they're rated for 100 lb. If

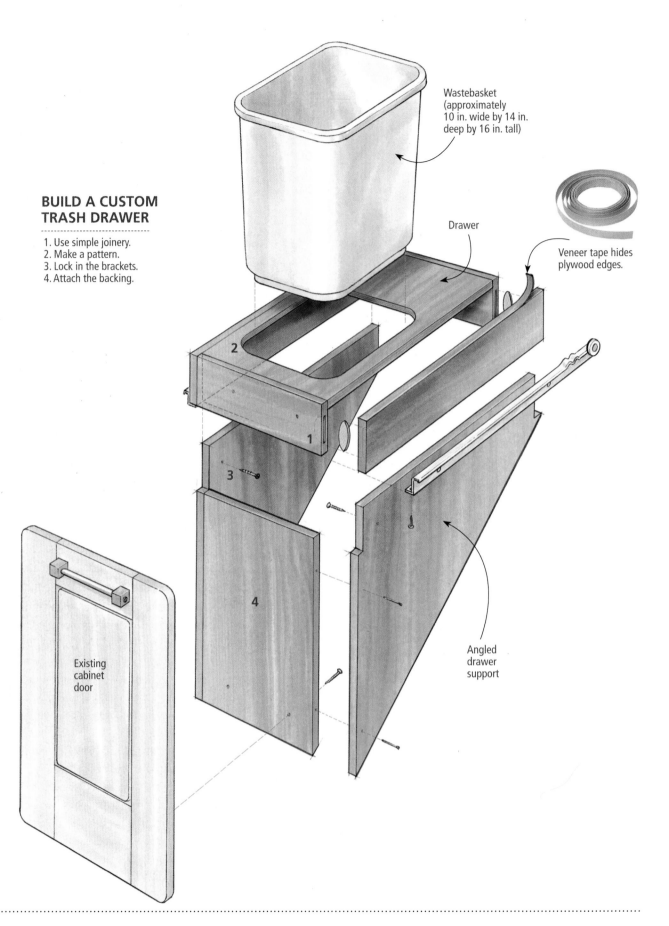

BUILD A CUSTOM TRASH DRAWER

1. Use simple joinery.
2. Make a pattern.
3. Lock in the brackets.
4. Attach the backing.

Wastebasket (approximately 10 in. wide by 14 in. deep by 16 in. tall)

Drawer

Veneer tape hides plywood edges.

Existing cabinet door

Angled drawer support

you choose a different type of slide, be sure to determine the necessary clearance before building the trash drawer.

Build the drawer

Made from ½-in. birch plywood, the trash unit is essentially a drawer turned upside down, reinforced with an angled support, and attached to the cabinet door. Start by cutting the sides for the drawer and joining them with biscuits.

Make a cardboard template that fits snugly beneath the outside rim of the wastebasket; the templated hole is traced onto the top. After drilling a hole for blade access, cut out the basket hole with a jigsaw. Use a 4-in-1 rasp or sandpaper to clean up the edges for a final fit. Nail and glue the top into place flush with the top edges of the drawer.

Support the door

Notch the angled drawer supports on the front and back so that they slide inside the drawer. Fasten them with 1-in. screws.

Cut the front panel, then glue and nail it between the angled supports. Drill four ¼-in. holes, two in the drawer front and two in the front panel for the screws that attach the drawer to the cabinet door.

Hang it in the cabinet

Before you install drawer slides, make a jig from ¼-in. medium-density fiberboard (MDF) or plywood. Drill holes that correspond to those on the slides, and attach the jig to a small block at one end. With the jig aligned to the slides' position, use an awl to start pilot holes for the mounting screws. Note: In face-frame cabinets, you can screw spacers to the cabinet sides as the author is doing here, or you can use a slide hanger, as seen on the back of the slide in the drawing on the facing page.

Drill ¼-in. holes in the drawer box's front face and near the bottom of the front panel. Attach heavy-duty double-stick carpet tape to the front of the unit. Lay shims of the intended reveal thickness (usually about ⅛ in.) along the bottom of the cabinet opening. Remove the backer on the tape, position the door on the shims, and push the door onto the tape. After checking the reveals on the sides, ease out the drawer, and screw the door to the unit from inside.

Rex Alexander is a kitchen designer and cabinetmaker in Fenton, Mich.

MAKE A DRAWER-SLIDE JIG. In ¼-in. medium-density fiberboard (MDF) or plywood, create a jig by drilling holes that correspond to those on the slides.

USE TAPE AND SHIMS TO INSTALL THE DOOR. To achieve the intended reveal, double-stick carpet tape and shims are used to position the door.

STANLEY.

LIVING & DINING ROOMS

Arts and Crafts Bookcase

BY ASA CHRISTIANA █ You can thank Mike Pekovich, *Fine Woodworking*'s art director, for designing this simple but handsome bookcase. He took a straightforward form—an oak bookcase with dado and rabbet joints—gave it nice proportions, and added a few elegant curves.

Pekovich and I agreed that screws would reinforce the joints well, and that gave us a design option on the sides. Choose oak plugs and align the grain carefully, and the plugs almost disappear. Make walnut or maple plugs instead, and the contrasting wood adds a nice design feature to the broad sides, highlighting the construction.

Before diving in, take a moment to appreciate a few of the subtler details. Curves add life to rectangular furniture, and this design uses three types of them, each irregular and organic, as opposed to radius curves that can seem mechanical.

10 EASY PIECES

The solid-wood parts are red oak, and the back is oak plywood. The parts are joined with simple rabbets and dadoes, reinforced by long screws. Shopmade plugs cover the screws.

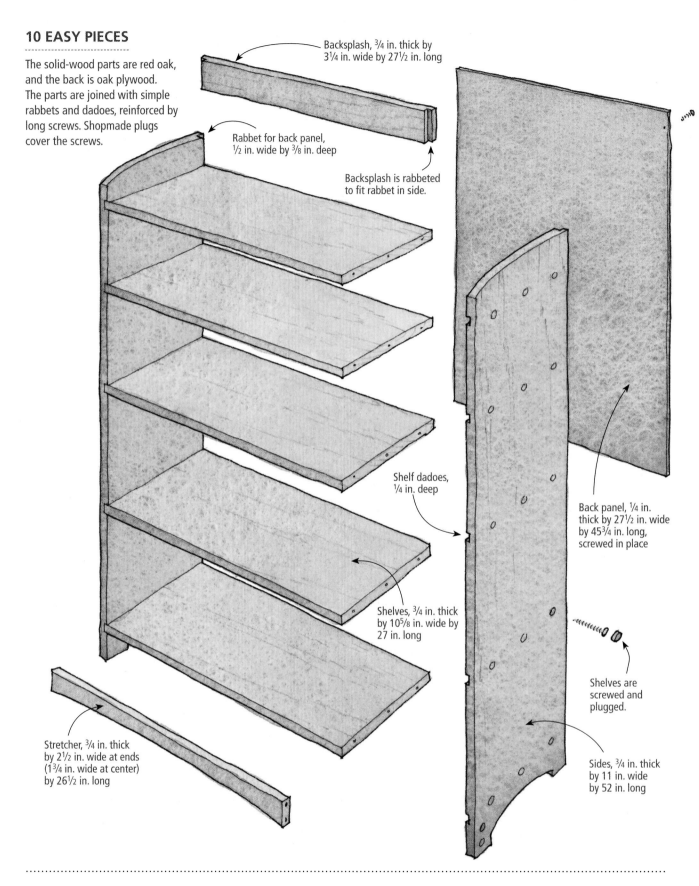

Backsplash, ¾ in. thick by 3¼ in. wide by 27½ in. long

Rabbet for back panel, ½ in. wide by ⅜ in. deep

Backsplash is rabbeted to fit rabbet in side.

Shelf dadoes, ¼ in. deep

Shelves, ¾ in. thick by 10⅝ in. wide by 27 in. long

Back panel, ¼ in. thick by 27½ in. wide by 45¾ in. long, screwed in place

Shelves are screwed and plugged.

Stretcher, ¾ in. thick by 2½ in. wide at ends (1¾ in. wide at center) by 26½ in. long

Sides, ¾ in. thick by 11 in. wide by 52 in. long

The top of each side has a gentle curve, drawn from a section of a French curve, that tightens as it moves forward. At the bottom are two natural curves formed with a flexible wood batten. On the stretcher, the curve extends end to end; the bottom of each side features a short, graceful arch that begins and ends with a straight step to suggest legs. Pekovich also made the sides and back extend up past the top of the case, creating a natural display area.

Last, note how the space between the shelves is graduated, growing smaller as it moves upward. This is common in bookcases because it is both pleasing to the eye and functional, creating a sense of movement and inviting different-size items onto different shelves.

Important lessons are built in

The bookcase is designed around a number of fundamental lessons for would-be furniture makers. The entire project can be completed with just a circular saw, jigsaw, drill, and a router. And if, as we did, you use the presurfaced lumber available at most home centers and lumberyards, you won't need pricey milling machines. Although it is cheaper to buy rough (oversize) lumber and mill it yourself, before investing in a jointer and a planer, you want to be sure you have the space for them, can handle the noise and dust, and will be using them more than a few times a year.

TO SEE OR NOT TO SEE. Make the plugs from a contrasting wood like walnut (photo, p. 45) to emphasize the construction. Or use the same wood as the rest of the piece to make the plugs disappear.

You can watch a complete series of free videos on how to build this bookcase at www.FineWoodworking.com/ quickprojects, but all of the information you'll need is also pictured in detail in the next pages.

Size the parts and cut the joinery

The construction is pretty straightforward. Start by picking flat and straight boards, and then cut all of the parts to size using a miter saw, circular saw, bandsaw, or better yet, a midsize tablesaw.

The shelves attach to the sides with simple dadoes, and the back panel and backsplash fit into rabbets. There are a lot of ways to cut these square notches in wood, but the easiest and most surefire method is to use a simple

LUMBER AND HARDWARE LIST

PART	QTY	SIZE	MATERIAL
Sides	2	³/₄ x 11 x 52	Oak
Shelves	5	³/₄ x 10⁵/₈ x 27	Oak
Backsplash	1	³/₄ x 3¹/₄ x 27¹/₂	Oak
Stretcher	1	³/₄ x 3 x 26¹/₂	Oak
Back panel	1	¹/₄ x 27¹/₂ x 45³/₄	Oak veneer, plywood
Screws for shelves, backsplash, stretcher	38	#12 x 2-in. flathead screws	Steel
Screws for back	24	#6 x ³/₄-in. flathead screws	Steel
Glue	1	8 fl. oz. bottle	Yellow glue

T-square jig to guide a handheld router through the dado cuts. To cut the rabbets in the back, I use the router's accessory edge guide to keep the cuts on track. Mark and then cut the curves in the sides and stretcher using either a bandsaw or jigsaw. You can smooth the pieces with a power sander or just use a hand sander—that would be you, armed with sandpaper and a sanding block.

Once the parts are sized and the profiles cut, you can lay out and drill the holes that attach through the sides and into the ends of shelves. The best way to avoid split wood and stripped screws is to drill right-size clearance and pilot holes in the sides and shelves (detail, p. 51).

I sanded most of the parts before gluing the piece. That way, I didn't have to sand into any corners or tight spaces after assembly. And when I did glue it all, the screws that strengthen the dado joints help to hold everything together while the glue dries, so I used fewer clamps. Add the plugs—which you can buy or make yourself with a bandsaw—at the end to fill those ugly screw holes.

I finished the piece using oil and wax.

BOOKCASE DIMENSIONS

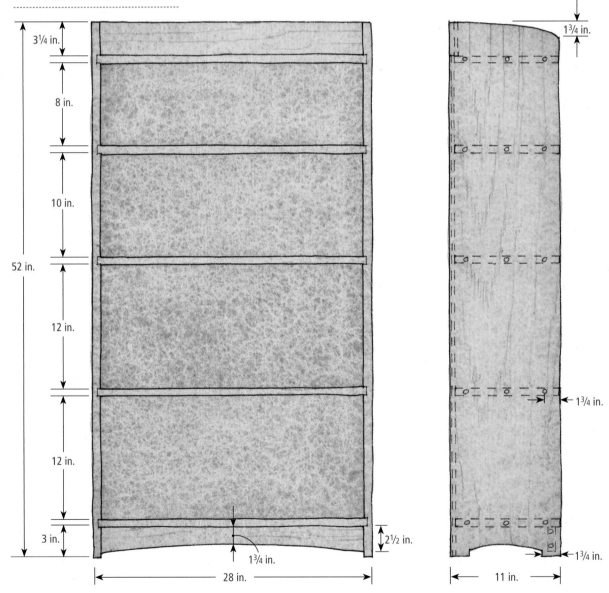

Cutting the Joinery

EYEING STRAIGHT BOARDS. If you're buying presurfaced boards, sight down the edges and faces to be sure they're straight. Twisting or warping are hard to fix without a jointer and planer.

TABLESAW SUPPORTS. Use a stand to balance long pieces when crosscutting to length. A well-positioned workbench can help support the pieces while ripping boards to length.

DADOES MADE EASY. Make a simple T-square jig for cutting dadoes with a handheld router. The jig has a fence that sits against the edge of a work-piece, and another that guides the router.

RABBETS, TOO. Use the router's edge-guide accessory to cut rabbets in the bookcase sides. Screwing an extra-long wood fence to the edge guide gives better control when entering the cut.

JIGSAW BASICS. The bookcase has a number of curves that can be cut with a jigsaw (shown) or a band-saw. The less-expensive jigsaw is a great tool for beginners.

SMOOTH CURVES. You can use a variety of tools to fair the curves. For outside curves, a small, handheld belt sander is the quicker option, but a sanding block will also work.

INSIDE CURVES CAN BE TRICKY. But a curved sanding block makes it easy. Make a block out of waste pieces from the jigsaw cuts. Keep the sandpaper in place with staples.

WHAT'S A COUNTERBORE? This larger hole creates a place for the screw head to sit below the surface. A plug on top will hide the screw. Use a Forstner bit for a big hole like this.

SMALL DRILL FOLLOWS BIG ONE. The Forstner bit leaves a little dimple in the center of the hole, which guides the smaller bit. The shaft of the screw passes freely through this clearance hole.

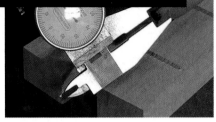

DIAL IN THE PILOT HOLE. Use a caliper to determine the size of your screw by measuring the root (between the threads) for the pilot hole. If you don't have a caliper, do it by eye.

DRY-FIT AND DRILL PILOT HOLES. To locate the pilot holes, fit the shelves into their dadoes and clamp the assembly. Keep the bit in the center of the clearance hole when drilling.

BRUSH ON THE GLUE. After dry-fitting the case and drilling the pilot holes, take apart the case and brush yellow glue on the joints, being sure to put glue on both mating surfaces.

CLAMP IT UP. Long parallel-jaw clamps are a good investment. They help keep assemblies square. Be sure the shelves stay flush with the front edges of the sides.

PLUG-CUTTER BASICS. If you have a drill press, you can use a plug-cutter to make your own plugs in any wood. Don't drill too deep or the plug will break off and jam in the cutter.

BANDSAW THEM FREE. This is an old boatbuilder's trick. If you have a bandsaw, just run the workpiece on edge to free the plugs. Then chase them around the shop floor.

TAP THEM HOME. You can test your counterbores in scrapwood to be sure they will be deep enough to hold the screw and plug. To insert a plug, just dip the tip in glue and tap it home.

A FEW FINAL PIECES. The backsplash is cut to length and rabbeted, and then glued and screwed in place. Cut the lower stretcher to fit between the sides and screw it in place.

EASY OIL FINISH. It's easier to finish the sides before attaching the rear panel. I sanded the pieces to P400 grit, and then applied three coats of tung oil, followed by a coat of paste wax.

Make the bookcase your own

Don't be afraid to make changes to this or any other project you see in magazines. There are other presurfaced woods at the lumberyard or home center—maple, pine, and even poplar, which works great if you plan to paint the piece. And if you have a jointer and planer, you can buy rough lumber at a hardwood dealer and choose from a wider selection of woods.

Feel free to change the size of the case, too. I'd still recommend graduating the shelves, though; it just looks better.

You can leave out the screws and plugs, too. If you screw the plywood back into its rabbets and to every shelf, it will add plenty of strength to the case.

If you are unfamiliar with any of the techniques, watch the online videos carefully. And when you're finished with the bookcase, be sure to let everyone know you built it. Bragging is half the fun.

Asa Christiana is the *Fine Woodworking* Special Projects Editor. Illustrations by Jim Richey.

A LOOK AT THE BACK

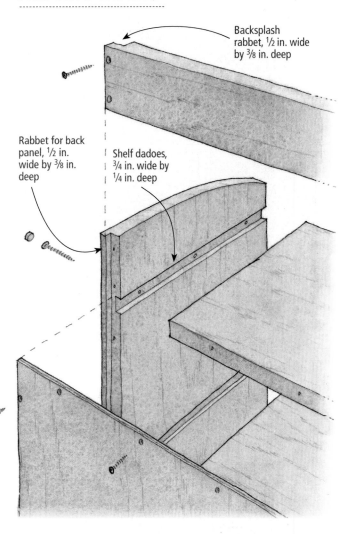

Backsplash rabbet, ½ in. wide by ⅜ in. deep

Rabbet for back panel, ½ in. wide by ⅜ in. deep

Shelf dadoes, ¾ in. wide by ¼ in. deep

Back is screwed in place.

FOOT DETAIL

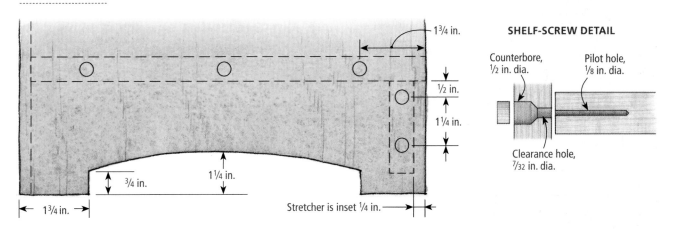

1¾ in.

½ in.

1¼ in.

1¼ in.

¾ in.

1¾ in.

Stretcher is inset ¼ in.

SHELF-SCREW DETAIL

Counterbore, ½ in. dia.

Pilot hole, ⅛ in. dia.

Clearance hole, ⁷⁄₃₂ in. dia.

Add Storage to Your Stair Rail

BY SCOTT GIBSON ▮ My friend Kevin took a long look at the makeshift railing at the top of the stairs and hesitated only slightly before asking, "Have you thought about turning that into a bookcase?" It was not so much a question but rather a suggestion I recognized immediately as requiring a ton of

FURNITURE-GRADE DETAILS FROM ALL ANGLES

Instead of a traditional railing, the author chose to enclose the open side of an office stairwell with a long bookcase. At 36 in. high, it meets code requirements, increases the room's storage capacity, and adds a new level of style. Cantilevered over the stairs, the bookcase occupies little floor space. A ledger and corbels provide decorative support.

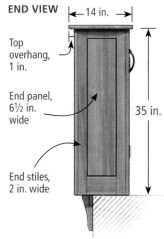

END VIEW

14 in.

Top overhang, 1 in.

End panel, 6½ in. wide

35 in.

End stiles, 2 in. wide

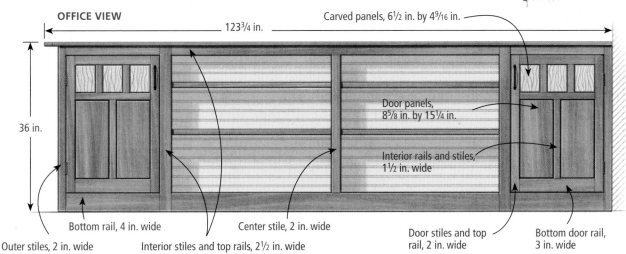

OFFICE VIEW

123¾ in.

Carved panels, 6½ in. by 4⁹⁄₁₆ in.

Door panels, 8⅝ in. by 15¼ in.

Interior rails and stiles, 1½ in. wide

36 in.

Bottom rail, 4 in. wide

Center stile, 2 in. wide

Door stiles and top rail, 2 in. wide

Bottom door rail, 3 in. wide

Outer stiles, 2 in. wide

Interior stiles and top rails, 2½ in. wide

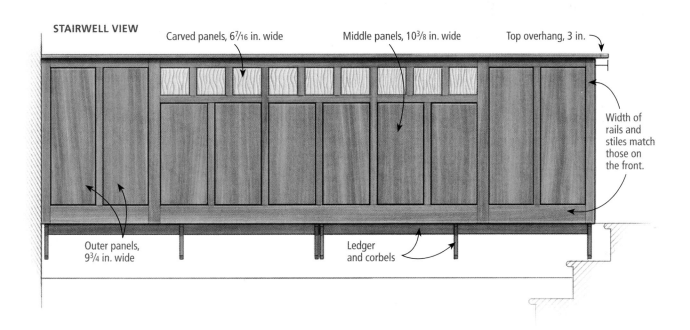

STAIRWELL VIEW

Carved panels, 6⁷⁄₁₆ in. wide

Middle panels, 10⅜ in. wide

Top overhang, 3 in.

Width of rails and stiles match those on the front.

Outer panels, 9¾ in. wide

Ledger and corbels

extra work. But it was also too good to ignore. My wife's home office is right next to the stairwell, and by substituting a bookcase for a traditional balustrade, I could provide lots of storage for books and office supplies.

I sketched some ideas until I arrived at one I liked. Facing my wife's work area, the cabinet would have two sections of open shelves for books flanked by cabinets concealed with doors. A frame-and-panel back would face the stairs. To save a few inches of floor space, the case would overhang the stairwell, resting on a ledger and a series of brackets.

The bookcase gives us 18 running ft. of shelf space, plus two cabinets nearly 2 ft. wide, while taking up about 6½ sq. ft. of floor space.

Make a long built-in manageable

The bookcase is only 1 ft. deep, but it's 10 ft. long. That posed some problems. I couldn't assemble and finish the project in place, and in my small shop, it wasn't practical to build the case as a single unit. So I divided it into two 5-ft.-long plywood boxes joined in the middle. Face frames on the front and back of the case, along with an MDF beadboard back, span the seam and give the case structural rigidity (drawings at right). The plywood cases are straightforward, assembled with #20 biscuits and 2-in. screws.

The only nonstandard detail is at the bottom of the bookcase, and it is something that normally would never be seen. Because this bookcase cantilevers into the stairwell, a strip of the finish wood several inches wide had to be let into the bottom of the case.

Before assembling the boxes, I cut the holes for shelf pins, and with help from

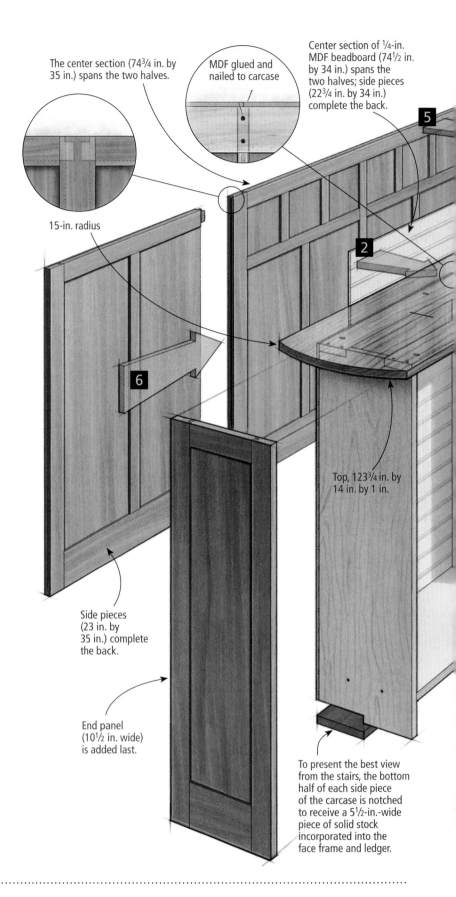

The center section (74¾ in. by 35 in.) spans the two halves.

15-in. radius

MDF glued and nailed to carcase

Center section of ¼-in. MDF beadboard (74½ in. by 34 in.) spans the two halves; side pieces (22¾ in. by 34 in.) complete the back.

Top, 123¾ in. by 14 in. by 1 in.

Side pieces (23 in. by 35 in.) complete the back.

End panel (10½ in. wide) is added last.

To present the best view from the stairs, the bottom half of each side piece of the carcase is notched to receive a 5½-in.-wide piece of solid stock incorporated into the face frame and ledger.

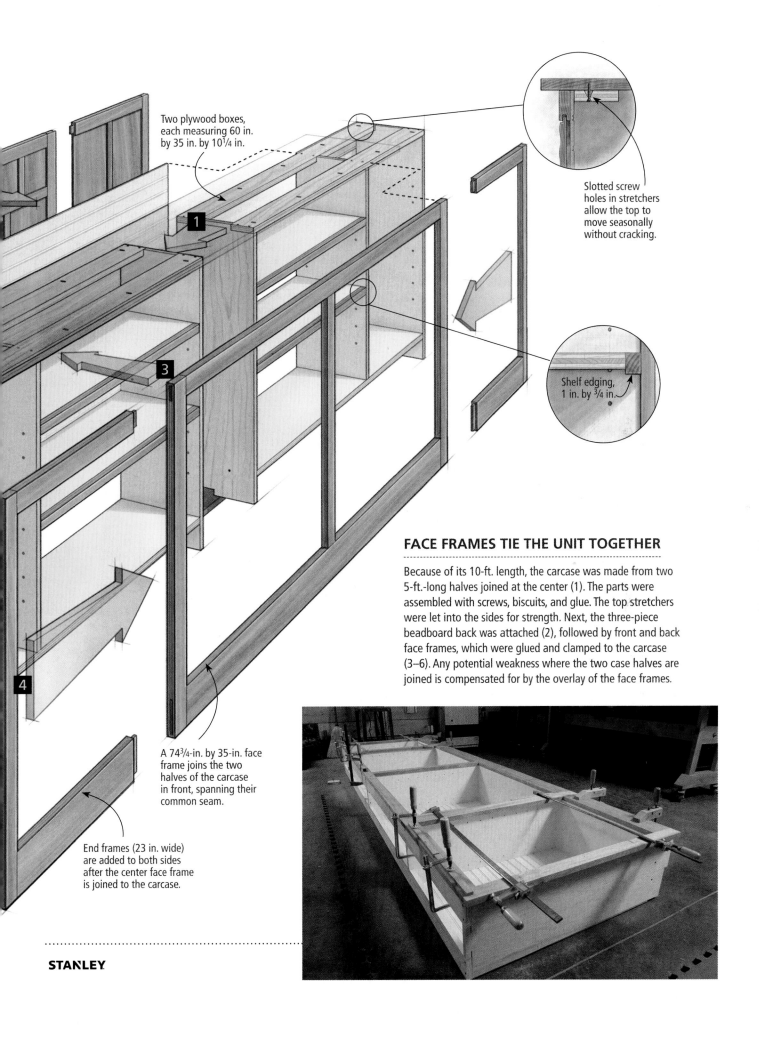

Two plywood boxes, each measuring 60 in. by 35 in. by 10¼ in.

1

3

4

Slotted screw holes in stretchers allow the top to move seasonally without cracking.

Shelf edging, 1 in. by ¾ in.

FACE FRAMES TIE THE UNIT TOGETHER

Because of its 10-ft. length, the carcase was made from two 5-ft.-long halves joined at the center (1). The parts were assembled with screws, biscuits, and glue. The top stretchers were let into the sides for strength. Next, the three-piece beadboard back was attached (2), followed by front and back face frames, which were glued and clamped to the carcase (3–6). Any potential weakness where the two case halves are joined is compensated for by the overlay of the face frames.

A 74¾-in. by 35-in. face frame joins the two halves of the carcase in front, spanning their common seam.

End frames (23 in. wide) are added to both sides after the center face frame is joined to the carcase.

TRADITIONAL JOINERY, WITH A WHIMSICAL VARIATION

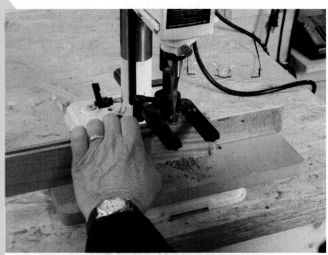

Mortise-and-tenon joints were used on the face frames and doors. The tenons were cut on a tablesaw, and the mortises were quickly excavated with a benchtop mortiser (top left). The haunched tenon adds strength and fills the exposed slot cut for panels.

The decorative panels were first cut, then secured between two stops. A router fitted with a ½-in. core-box bit was used to free-hand the designs (bottom left). The panels were given two coats of paint before they were incorporated into the frames.

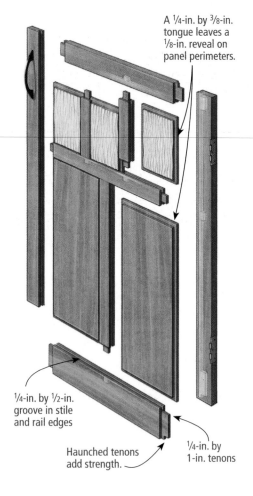

A ¼-in. by ⅜-in. tongue leaves a ⅛-in. reveal on panel perimeters.

¼-in. by ½-in. groove in stile and rail edges

Haunched tenons add strength.

¼-in. by 1-in. tenons

my wife, Susan, painted all interior surfaces. Painter's tape kept biscuit slots free of paint.

With the cases clamped together temporarily, I took all the measurements I needed for the face frames. Then I pushed the cases out of the way and got to work on the face frames.

Add interest with small, textured, decorative panels

Like the carcase, the face frames were built in sections. To join the boxes, the front and back of the case got a 6-ft.-wide face frame in the center. Then each end got a smaller face frame, roughly 2 ft. wide on the ends.

Cutting mortises and tenons is an antiquated approach in the era of the Kreg pocket-hole jig, but the joinery is reliable and strong. The wood is utile, a West African hardwood often used as a substitute for South American mahogany. It has some attractive ribbon stripping, machines well, and sands and finishes nicely.

To break up the monotony of all that utile on the section facing the stairwell, I introduced nine small panels, each about 6 in. square. I added texture to the face of each panel with the tip of a 1/2-in. core-box router bit, painted the panels the same color as the cabinet interior, and sanded them lightly to let some of the wood show through. I used the same panels to dress up the doors on the office-facing side of the bookcase.

Before gluing up the paneled section facing the stairs, I finished any edges that would be inaccessible. After the section was glued up, I pinned the panels in place from the back side with small nails, one nail in the middle of each panel top and bottom. The pins let the panels move with changes in humidity but keep them centered.

Glue-up is challenging

With the two big face-frame sections assembled and the rest of the parts and pieces milled, I was ready to give up the floor space in my shop and put the carcase together. I screwed together the two plywood boxes, tipped the case on its face, and attached the center piece of MDF bead-board with glue and nails. Then I rolled the case on its back and glued on the first frame.

PAINT FIRST, THEN ASSEMBLE. Prime and paint interior surfaces before assembly. Use painter's tape to keep paint from clogging biscuit slots. Also, cut or drill holes for adjustable shelving.

In advance, I'd milled mortises in the stiles on each end of the center frame so that the other pieces could be added in sections: first the 6-ft.-wide center section, then the wings on each side. Building the case this way meant I didn't have to handle or machine any pieces of lumber much longer than 75 in.

When the case had a complete front face frame, I repeated the process on the back: first the preassembled frame-and-panel center section, then the two end frames and their panels. Then I sanded down everything and finished it with a wipe-on polyurethane finish.

I left the doors and top for later to reduce the weight of the case, and with some borrowed muscle, I moved the case out of the shop, into the house, and then up the stairs.

Add brackets, and install the case

With only one-third of the case cantilevered over the stairwell, most of the bookcase's weight is supported by the floor. But to prevent the case from tipping, I installed a ledger and five corbels. The 1-in.-thick, 7½-in.-long corbels are notched, glued, and screwed to the ledger. The ledger is screwed to the face of the stairwell opening.

The bookcase abuts a wall at the far end of the stairwell, and here, I ran screws through the end and then into the wall framing to anchor it. To set the rest of the bookcase, I ran long screws through the bottom of the case into the floor; then I plugged the counterbores and touched up the paint.

When the rest of the rail system for the stairs is installed, I'll tie the bookcase to the post at the top of the stairs.

Scott Gibson, a contributing writer to *Fine Homebuilding*, lives in Southern Maine. Photos courtesy of the author. Illustrations by John Hartman.

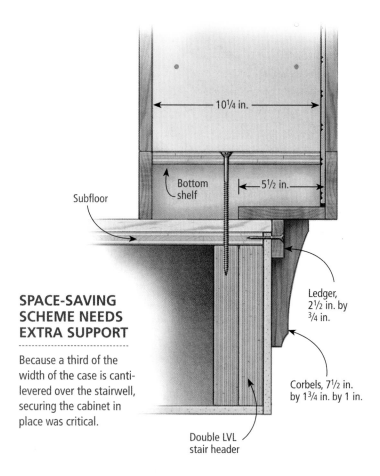

10¼ in.

Subfloor

Bottom shelf

5½ in.

Ledger, 2½ in. by ¾ in.

Corbels, 7½ in. by 1¾ in. by 1 in.

Double LVL stair header

SPACE-SAVING SCHEME NEEDS EXTRA SUPPORT

Because a third of the width of the case is cantilevered over the stairwell, securing the cabinet in place was critical.

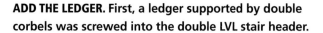

ADD THE LEDGER. First, a ledger supported by double corbels was screwed into the double LVL stair header.

SECURE THE CASE. After the case was moved into position, 6-in. by ⁵⁄₁₆-in. screws were driven through the cabinet into the subflooring and, where possible, the framing. The end opposite the top of the stairs was screwed into the wall framing as well.

Straight-Ahead Corner Hutch

BY GARY STRIEGLER ▪ A built-in corner hutch takes advantage of space that often goes unused. It also softens the feel of a room while adding architectural interest. I like this hutch because its finished appearance doesn't betray the fact that it's easy and affordable to build. The carcase, face frame, and shelves are made from ¾-in. medium-density fiberboard (MDF), and the trim details can be created with stock profiles.

The hutch's scale should match the room's scale. For dining rooms, I've found that 42 in. across the face frame provides good shelf depth while maintaining a manageable size that won't intrude on the room. For trim details, I use a selection of stock profiles that give the hutch a classic

CONT'D ON PAGE 62 ▶

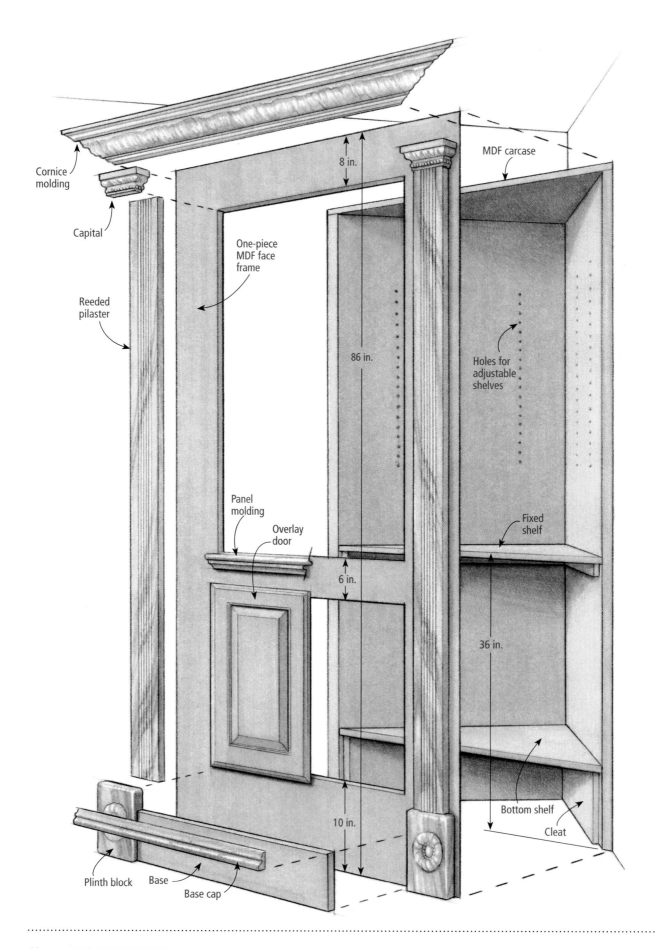

Cornice molding

Capital

Reeded pilaster

One-piece MDF face frame

Panel molding

Overlay door

Plinth block

Base

Base cap

MDF carcase

Holes for adjustable shelves

Fixed shelf

Bottom shelf

Cleat

8 in.

86 in.

6 in.

36 in.

10 in.

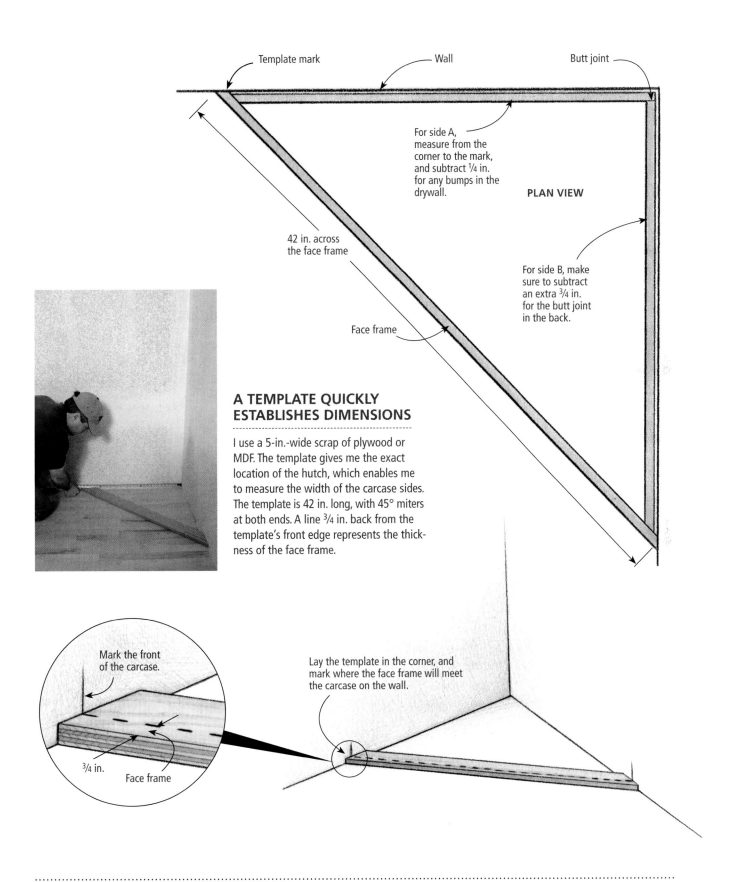

Template mark

Wall

Butt joint

For side A, measure from the corner to the mark, and subtract 1/4 in. for any bumps in the drywall.

PLAN VIEW

42 in. across the face frame

Face frame

For side B, make sure to subtract an extra 3/4 in. for the butt joint in the back.

A TEMPLATE QUICKLY ESTABLISHES DIMENSIONS

I use a 5-in.-wide scrap of plywood or MDF. The template gives me the exact location of the hutch, which enables me to measure the width of the carcase sides. The template is 42 in. long, with 45° miters at both ends. A line 3/4 in. back from the template's front edge represents the thickness of the face frame.

Mark the front of the carcase.

3/4 in.

Face frame

Lay the template in the corner, and mark where the face frame will meet the carcase on the wall.

feel: crown molding, reeded pilasters on plinth blocks, and panel molding all simply applied to the face frame.

The one-piece face frame is the biggest time-saver in this project. This detail eliminates the work needed to assemble the frame from separate stiles and rails.

Carcase goes together quickly

With its simple construction and straightforward joinery, the carcase for the hutch comes together in no time. The two sides are held together by two triangular shelves and a top. The shelves are fastened to cleats, and the top is glued and screwed to the sides from above.

1 **RIP THE SIDES. I tilt the saw base to a 45° bevel and rip the sides, guiding the circular saw against a straight length of MDF.**

2 **FASTEN THE SHELVES. The fixed shelves are fastened to MDF cleats. To join the sides, I use a simple butt joint screwed from the back.**

3 **MOVE THE CARCASE INTO PLACE. When the carcase is done, I plumb and shim it between the layout marks I made on the wall. The hutch is attached to the framing with a 3-in. screw in each wall near the top of the carcase.**

No joinery

MDF is stable and sturdy, and it takes paint well. I can save time and money by cutting the face frame from a single piece of MDF. Since the face frame is a single piece, it requires no complicated and time-consuming joinery.

1 **CUT THE OPENINGS IN THE FACE FRAME WITH A CIRCULAR SAW.** I use a plunge cut guided by a straightedge. In the corners, I finish the cut with a handsaw or a jigsaw.

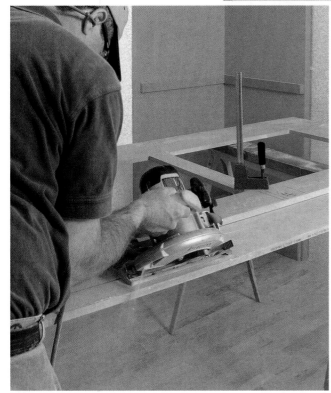

2 **CUT THE SIDES OF THE FACE FRAME AT A 47° BEVEL.** This makes for a snug fit against the wall and the front of the carcase. For this hutch, I used an 8-in. border on the sides of the face frame. Anything smaller starts to compromise the strength, and anything larger looks clunky and awkward.

3 **TILT THE FACE FRAME INTO PLACE.** I make the bottom shelf flush with the face frame, then attach it to the case with 15-ga. finish nails.

Final touches define the look

Stock trim details give this hutch a classic look. I used crown, capitals, plinths, pilasters, and panel molding. I softened the corner by adding a 5-in.-wide panel in the back and refined the look with a simple beaded molding around the upper opening. Your local door and window supplier should have a good selection of trim profiles. Online, you can find a nearly limitless variety of embossed and shaped trim profiles. Just remember that the trim, the door design, and the style of the room all should work together to create a unified look.

Gary Striegler, a frequent contributor to *Fine Homebuilding*, is a custom-home builder in Fayetteville, Ark. He teaches each summer at the Marc Adams School of Woodworking and works with Mercy International on building projects in Honduras. Photo p. 59 by Rick Green. Illustrations by Bob La Pointe.

1 **ADD THE MOLDING.** The crown, capitals, plinths, pilasters, and panel molding I used are from White River Hardwoods (www.mouldings.com).

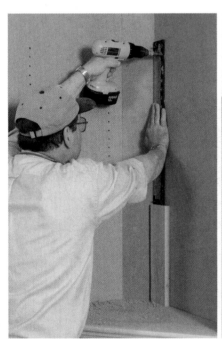

2 **DRILL FOR THE SHELVES.** To bore holes for shelf-support pins, I use a self-centering bit and a drilling jig from Rockler® (www.rockler.com).

3 **BUY OR BUILD THE DOORS.** I took the MDF door blanks for this hutch to a local cabinet shop, where a CNC machine milled the profiles. You can build the doors yourself, or you can order them from online suppliers (www.scherrs.com; www.lakesidemoulding.com).

FACE-MOUNT CUP HINGE. Compared to edge-mount cup hinges (photo, left), face-mount, overlay-style cup hinges provide a stronger connection and a cleaner look. The Blum hinge shown here is from Woodcraft® (#02R80; www.woodcraft.com).

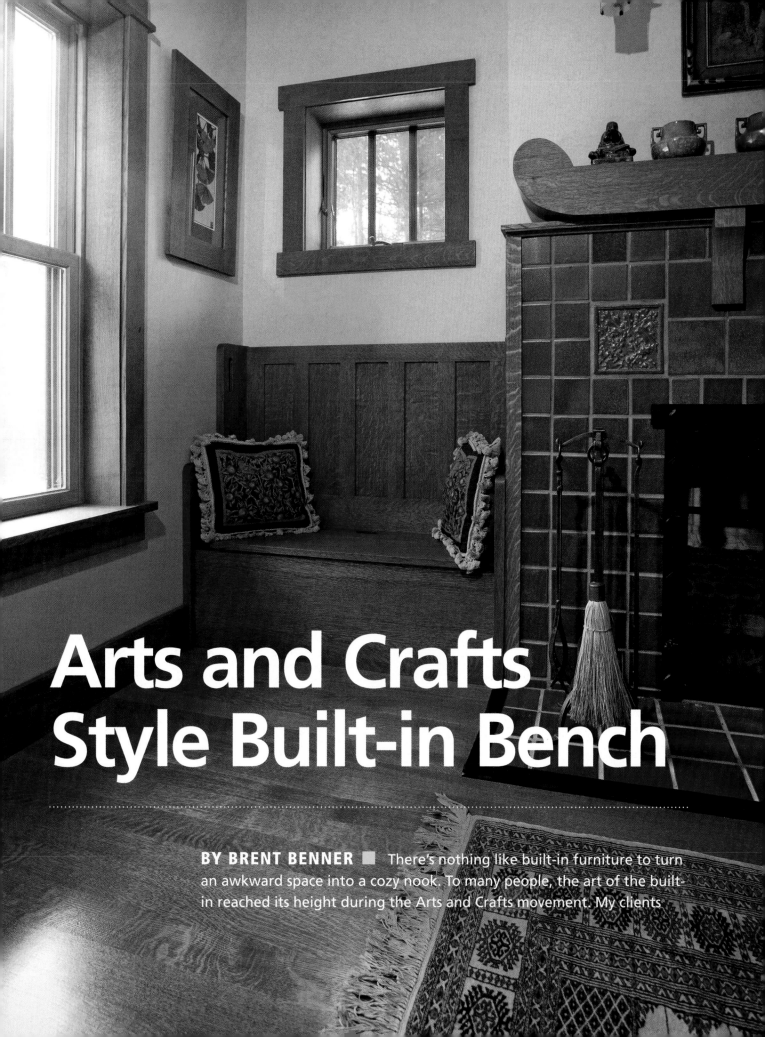

Arts and Crafts
Style Built-in Bench

BY BRENT BENNER ▪ There's nothing like built-in furniture to turn an awkward space into a cozy nook. To many people, the art of the built-in reached its height during the Arts and Crafts movement. My clients

ASSEMBLY WITH FLEXIBILITY IN MIND

This bench is essentially a box within a box. The inner box is stable plywood, and the outer is white oak, which like most solid wood tends to move seasonally. The various parts of the bench have to be assembled with elongated screw holes so that the wood won't crack when it swells or shrinks. Because it's a built-in, the bench also must have extra material in key areas so that it can be scribed to the floor and walls.

The dadoes that accept the back are stopped about 1½ in. below the top edge so that they won't show; the back stiles are notched accordingly.

The back panels are captured (but not glued) by stiles and rails joined with a ¼-in. by ⁵⁄₁₆-in. stub tenon and a ¼-in. by ³⁄₈-in. groove.

A ³⁄₄-in. by ³⁄₄-in. piece of oak conceals the top front edge of the plywood box when the seat is open.

26³⁄₄ in.

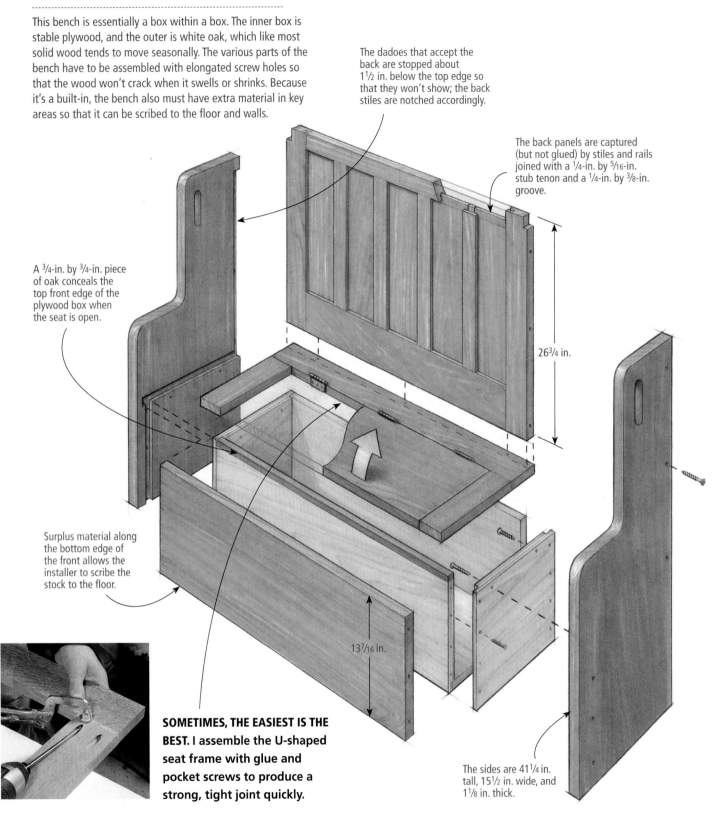

Surplus material along the bottom edge of the front allows the installer to scribe the stock to the floor.

13⁷⁄₁₆ in.

SOMETIMES, THE EASIEST IS THE BEST. I assemble the U-shaped seat frame with glue and pocket screws to produce a strong, tight joint quickly.

The sides are 41¼ in. tall, 15½ in. wide, and 1⅛ in. thick.

hold that opinion so dear to their hearts that they've turned their house into a showcase of period design. Recently, they asked me to build an Arts and Crafts style bench to serve as an inglenook for their living-room fireplace.

The bench began with a design borrowed from a similar piece in my clients' furniture collection. Made of quartersawn white oak, my take on the design has simple L-shaped sides with a decorative slot, a frame-and-panel backrest, and storage under a hinged seat. Like all good inglenooks, it's shoehorned into a space between the fireplace and a corner.

Start with accurate measurements

To determine the dimensions of the bench, I used a set of homemade measuring sticks to size the space where the bench would be installed. Nothing more than two

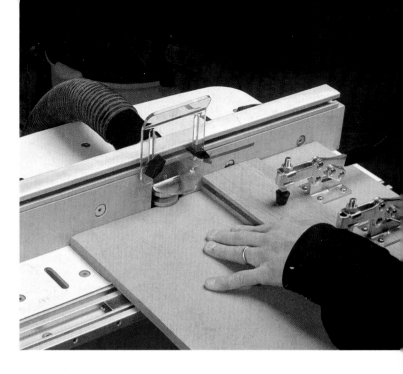

STUB TENONS. I cut the tenons with a double slot cutter and secured the stock on a shop-built crosscut sled. Hold-downs immobilize the stock, and a T-slot insert from a bevel guide keeps the jig parallel to the bit.

BUILD THE BACK PANEL LIKE A DOOR

I used a router table to shape the rails, stiles, and back panels. After cutting the stock to length, I routed the grooves with a ¼-in. slot cutter. Next, I cut the stub tenons with a double slot cutter. Finally, I used a vertical raised-panel bit to relieve the ¾-in.-thick panels' back side.

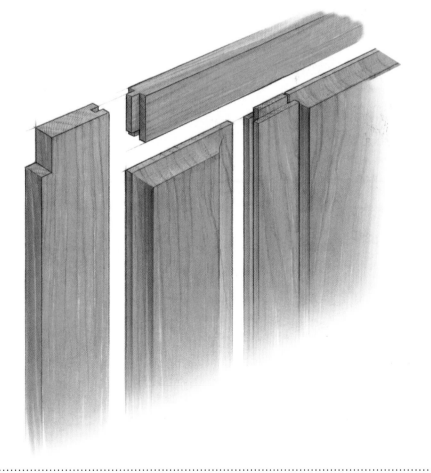

CUT SIDE PIECES WITH A TEMPLATE. The most accurate method of cutting identical pieces is to use a template. Here, I cut the design from a piece of ¼-in. medium-density fiberboard (MDF), traced its shape onto the side stock, then rough-cut the shape on a bandsaw. I used double-sided tape to adhere the template temporarily to the bottom of the stock and a 1½-in.-long down-shear flush-trim bit to trim to the line.

long pieces of 1x scrap wood held side by side, the sticks were telescoped out to the left and right to span the exact width of the space allotted for the bench. A pencil line drawn across both sticks marked the measurements that I later transferred to the bench design.

Once I had accurate site measurements, I made a shop drawing of the piece, and used the dimensions to mill and glue up stock for the sides, seat, and panels. I used 6/4 stock for the sides and 4/4 stock for the back; the final thicknesses came to 1⅛ in. and $^{13}/_{16}$ in., respectively. (If you don't have the tools to mill rough-sawn lumber, most local hardwood suppliers can plane and joint stock for a small fee.)

After all the parts were milled, I began building the bench, starting with the back. Made like a cabinet door, the back is a frame-and-panel assembly; the rails and stiles are milled with a square-edged stub-tenon-and-groove joint. The panels aren't glued to the frame, so they can move seasonally. I made the panels ¾ in. thick so that they'd never crack or rattle in the frame, and I used a

TWO WAYS TO REDUCE TEAROUT

USE UP- AND DOWN-SHEAR BITS

Unlike straight router bits, whose flutes are parallel to the bit's shank, up-shear and down-shear bits have flutes that wrap helically around the bit. Down shear prevents tearout on the top surface; up shear prevents tearout at the bottom.

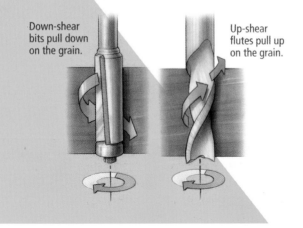

Down-shear bits pull down on the grain.

Up-shear flutes pull up on the grain.

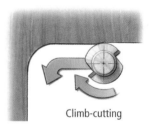

Standard router direction

Climb-cutting

CHANGE THE DIRECTION OF CUT

When routing, the accepted practice is to push the router against the direction of the bit's spin. When handheld, the router should travel from left to right; on a router table, the work is pushed from right to left. However, for handheld routing shapes that involve changes in grain direction or end-grain cuts, it's better to push the router in the opposite direction, a technique known as climb-cutting. For safety's sake, light passes and a firm grip on the router are recommended.

raised-panel bit to relieve the panels' edge to fit into the frame's groove. Although the raised profile is hidden on the back of the bench, the detail is historically accurate. When I had the back glued up, I built the box for the bench's storage space from ¾-in.-thick maple plywood.

Use templates for consistency

Next, I created a template that was the exact replica of the side pieces. I used ¼-in. MDF for the templates because it's inexpensive and uniform. Once the template was drawn and cut, I traced its outline onto the side stock, rough-cut the pieces on a bandsaw, then cleaned up the line using the template to guide a router and a flush-trim bit, which I've found makes a cleaner cut than a straight bit and bushing.

After cutting the decorative slots in the sides (also using a template), I routed dadoes to accept the seat apron and

1 **CLEAN DETAILS. To cut the decorative slot on the sides, I traced the outline of the slot, then drilled a ⅞-in. access hole with a Forstner bit, clamped the template to the back side of the stock, and began the cut with a top-bearing pattern bit.**

2 **FINISH THE CUT. I made successively deeper cuts until there was width enough to support a router bit's bearing from the opposite side. I removed the template, flipped over the stock, and used the down-shear flush-cutting bit to finish.**

3 **SECOND TEMPLATE. Because the cuts meet in the middle of the stock, the slot has sharp edges on both sides and a clean interior. I used a second template to cut dadoes in the bench sides for the seat frame and the front panel. This time, I used a bushing in the router base to guide an up/down spiral bit that cuts a flat-bottom dado and still doesn't produce any tearout on the surface.**

the seat. I used the original template to check the layout but made a new template to cut the dadoes. This time, I used a bushing attached to the router base that rides on the template; an up/down spiral bit removed the stock. This bit's down-shear cut limited tearout at the top of the cut, and the up-shear action on the tip cut a clean, flat bottom. I used the same setup to cut the rabbet for the back panel.

The last assembly I made was the seat and its frame, which was butt-jointed and pocket-screwed together. After trimming the seat to fit in the frame, I mortised and attached three 2½-in. brass hinges.

Because most of the fasteners are concealed, I used screws to assemble the bench. Before assembly, I used a ¼-in. drill bit to elongate the screw holes; the slightly larger elliptical hole allows the screw head to move as the wood moves and reduces the chance that the wood will crack. Finally, I dry-assembled the plywood box, the box front, the seat frame, the back, and the sides to check the fit, then repeated the assembly with glue and screws.

1 **ACCOUNT FOR MOVEMENT. By angling the drill back and forth, I enlarged the holes so that the screws could move with the wood as it expands and contracts seasonally.**

2 **ADJUST THE FIT. I checked the fit of the dadoes and made adjustments as needed.**

3 **GET READY FOR GLUE-UP. The back panels were notched to fit the stepped dadoes.**

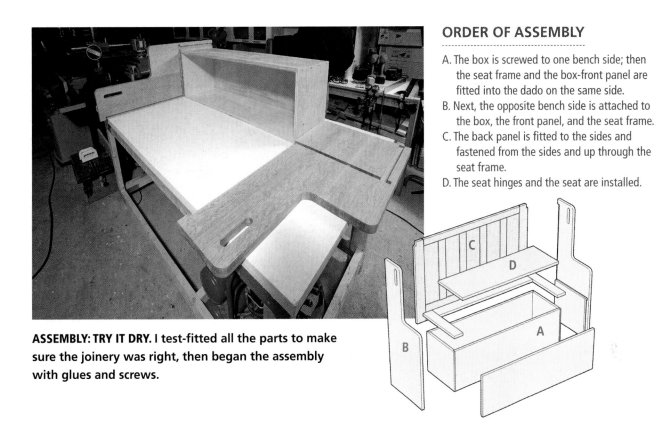

ORDER OF ASSEMBLY

A. The box is screwed to one bench side; then the seat frame and the box-front panel are fitted into the dado on the same side.
B. Next, the opposite bench side is attached to the box, the front panel, and the seat frame.
C. The back panel is fitted to the sides and fastened from the sides and up through the seat frame.
D. The seat hinges and the seat are installed.

ASSEMBLY: TRY IT DRY. I test-fitted all the parts to make sure the joinery was right, then began the assembly with glues and screws.

A combination of stains makes a realistic finish

The historically correct way to finish an Arts and Crafts piece involves ammonia fumes. Lucky for me, the home-owners had come up with an alternative they liked for other parts of the house, so I tried it on the bench. The first layer of stain was a stock Sherwin-Williams® variety (Cinnamon mixed in a Fruitwood base; www.sherwin-williams.com) that darkened the grain and added depth. After a few minutes, I wiped off the excess stain, lightly sanded the bench with a 220-grit foam sanding pad, cleaned it with a tack cloth, and repeated the process with a second coat of stain. This time, it was Benjamin Moore®'s Red Oak stain (www.benjaminmoore.com). I finished the bench with three coats of Benjamin Moore flat polyurethane, sanding lightly between coats.

To install the bench, I eased it into the space, leveled it, and scribed it to the floor. On the wall side of the bench, I had to back-bevel the side with a belt sander until it fit the wall tightly. On the fireplace side, a piece of ½-in. plywood covered the wall, so I shimmed it to meet the

FLOOD AND WIPE FOR A SUBTLE EFFECT. Applying the first coat of stain with a brush saturates the wood with color. After letting it sit for a minute, I wipe off the excess with an absorbent cloth. This first color provides a base tone that gives depth and character to the final color.

bench. The plywood edge later would be covered by the fireplace surround. I finished by securing the bench with screws through the plywood box and into the wall studs behind it.

Brent Benner is a cabinetmaker who lives and works in Roxbury, Conn. His website is www.roxburycabinet.com. All illustrations by Bob La Pointe, except for the illustration above by Taunton staff.

A Built-in Corner Seating Nook

BY JOSEPH LANZA　　My friends Debbie and Tom decided to make better use of a small room next to their kitchen. They wanted a built-in seat that could serve as an informal dining area and a place for board games or homework.

After measuring the space and designing the seat in cross section, I made a SketchUp model of a seat with enough room for four people, storage drawers below, and a cabinet in the back of the corner seat. Tom and Debbie liked the design, but before I started building, I made a 24-in.-wide plywood mock-up to make sure they would be comfortable sitting in it. We agreed that the mock-up was more comfortable with a ¾-in. plywood block under the front edge. I gave the seat an additional 5° tilt, then made a new SketchUp model of the base of the seat.

Because I would be working alone, building the seat in the shop and installing it as a complete unit were out of the question. Even if I had the strength to do so, the house was built in the 18th century, so plumb, level, and square had long since vanished. Because there was sure to be lots of scribing and fitting before the seat was in place, it made sense to break down the job into manageable parts. I decided to start with a level plinth, then to install the base as four separate boxes. Next, I would install the seat and the corner-cabinet unit, and then finish up with all of the solid-wood parts (the seat back, nosings, and moldings). I could make all the parts in the shop, then assemble everything together at the house.

Build boxes to form the seat

For the boxes below the seat, I used dimensions from the SketchUp model to cut parts from ¾-in. birch plywood. Because the seat has a 10° pitch, the joint between the cabinets at the top is a compound miter. To cut the joints, I used a circular saw with the blade set to a 3.81° bevel and a shooting board. The bevel angle came from a chart I found online (www.woodshoptips.com/tips/012003/012003.pdf). I cut the corner cabinet to the dimensions on the SketchUp model, but I made the two adjoining cabinets 1 in. longer so that I would have room to scribe and fit the joints in place.

Next, using a dado and rabbet joint that was glued and nailed, I made drawers from ½-in. Baltic-birch plywood. I delayed making the applied drawer fronts until the boxes and the face frames were in place and I could get an accurate measurement.

While in the shop, I ripped ¾-in. pine plywood to 16 in. for the seats. The back just overlaps the back edge of the seat. I also milled other parts, such as the solid-pine roun-

dover nosing for the seat, the pine grooved paneling, the face frame, and the cap stock.

Playing by old-house rules

Once on-site, my first task was to install the plinth, which is essentially a plywood box 3½ in. high that is analogous to a cabinet's toe kick. Starting at the high point, I leveled each side across, shimming with blocks and screwing the base to the baseboard. I hid the plywood and the gaps with a 1x pine kick board that I scribed to the floor.

The corner base unit was next. I marked left and right reference points an equal distance from the inside corner, then centered the corner base between the two points and screwed it to the plinth. Next, I scribed each of the flanking base units to the corner, checked the fit, and pocket-screwed the top edges together. I also screwed them together at the sides and into the walls.

THE CRITICAL ANGLES

Unlike a built-in or a set of stairs, a bench might look fine on paper, but the real test is whether it feels comfortable. A short mock-up built of plywood gives both the designer and the client a good sense of the bench's ergonomics.

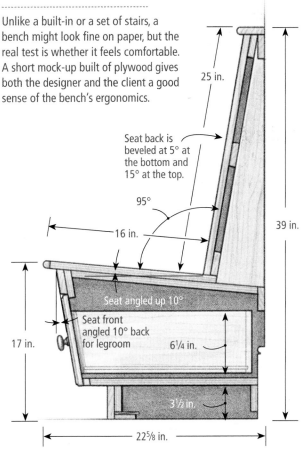

25 in.

Seat back is beveled at 5° at the bottom and 15° at the top.

95°

16 in.

39 in.

Seat angled up 10°

17 in.

Seat front angled 10° back for legroom

6¼ in.

3½ in.

22⅝ in.

JOIN BASE UNITS WITH A COMPOUND ANGLE

Begin with a level framework of plinth boxes. The plywood seat bases sit atop the plinth boxes and will eventually house drawers. Because the seat is angled back, the corner boxes are joined with a 22.5° angle and an approximately 4° bevel.

A SCRIBE MAY BE NECESSARY. Position the opposite side base, and check the fit. Use a set of scribes to mark the cut.

A SAW GUIDE IS A MUST. When trimming scribed cuts, a site-built saw guide is a fast way to make an accurate cut.

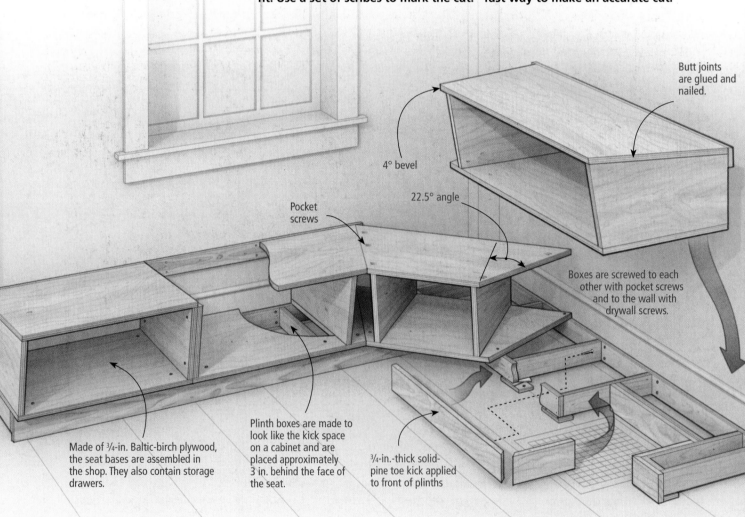

Butt joints are glued and nailed.

4° bevel

22.5° angle

Pocket screws

Boxes are screwed to each other with pocket screws and to the wall with drywall screws.

Made of ¾-in. Baltic-birch plywood, the seat bases are assembled in the shop. They also contain storage drawers.

Plinth boxes are made to look like the kick space on a cabinet and are placed approximately 3 in. behind the face of the seat.

¾-in.-thick solid-pine toe kick applied to front of plinths

The next part of the puzzle was the corner seat back. Built in the shop, the unit doubles as a storage cabinet. The idea was to use the storage unit as a reference when it came time to frame the rest of the seat back. I positioned the corner unit so that it was parallel to the front and level, then toe-screwed it to the seat and to the wall.

I opted to fit and install the plywood seat panels first, then have the seat back land on the seat. Otherwise, I'd have to scribe the seat to the back, leaving a visible joint. Beveled to the same angles as the seat base, the panels were ripped at 16 in. wide and cut to length to form an equal overhang at the front and sides. I attached the panels with screws driven up through the base.

The seat-back frame is a custom fit

Because the walls were not flat or plumb, I began making the seat-back frame with a series of triangular plywood panels connected by 1x4s. Notched over a ledger, the triangles' bases were screwed to the seat bases. Next,

I attached horizontal 1x4s across the top, middle, and bottom as nailers for the beadboard seat back. After both sides were complete, I covered the corner unit with a face frame.

Once these parts were fit and nailed up, I filled in the rest of the seat back, choosing the appropriate widths to fit the space. The right side went quickly, but the left was complicated by a window. There, I had to notch the first piece and lower a few more to make room for a small shelf below the windowsill.

When the back was complete, I glued and nailed the nosing to the front and side edges of the seat. Below the seat, I covered the veneer edges of the plywood with 1x solid stock, then filled in the face frames in the corners and above the drawers. After mounting the drawers on full-extension slides, I cut and fit the drawer fronts. Then I finished the beadboard paneling on the ends of the unit and added the final face-frame piece.

To cap it off, I started with a piece of ¾-in. pine plywood, which I fit into the corner by tick-sticking. I then scribed solid cap pieces to the wall along each side,

1 INSTALL THE CORNER CABINET. Centered plumb and level in the corner, the corner cabinet in part anchors the framing for the seat back and establishes the width of the seat.

2 FIT THE PLYWOOD SEAT PANELS. Start by locating the corner piece, which determines the location of the adjacent panels. After being scribed to fit, the panels are clamped in place and attached with screws driven from below.

ADD THE CORNER CABINET, SEAT PANELS, AND BACK FRAME

Built in the shop, the corner storage cabinet is installed on top of the seat bases, followed by the finished seat panels. To establish the top of the seat-back frame, a 1x3 ledger strip is screwed to the wall on the right. A framework of 1x pine is installed to create backing for the tongue-and-groove paneling.

The corner cabinet is installed first, followed by the seat panels. To establish the top of the seat-back frame, a ledger strip is screwed to the wall on the right.

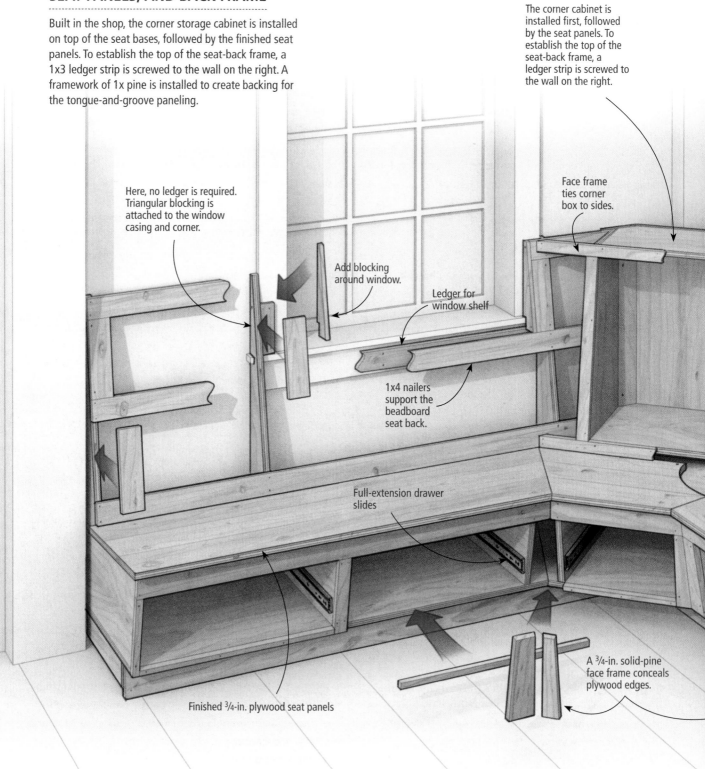

Here, no ledger is required. Triangular blocking is attached to the window casing and corner.

Add blocking around window.

Ledger for window shelf

Face frame ties corner box to sides.

1x4 nailers support the beadboard seat back.

Full-extension drawer slides

Finished ³⁄₄-in. plywood seat panels

A ³⁄₄-in. solid-pine face frame conceals plywood edges.

butting them to the side of the plywood and mitering them where they met the nosing on the front edge. I hung the doors on the corner unit with full-overlay cup hinges and fit a quirked bead against the face frame around them. Finally, I cleaned up my pencil marks and finish-sanded the unit. After I left, the painter came in and applied oil-based stain, sealed it with a coat of shellac, and brushed on two coats of polyurethane.

Joseph Lanza (www.josephlanza.com) designs and builds entire houses, as well as their parts, in Duxbury, Mass. Illustrations by John Hartman.

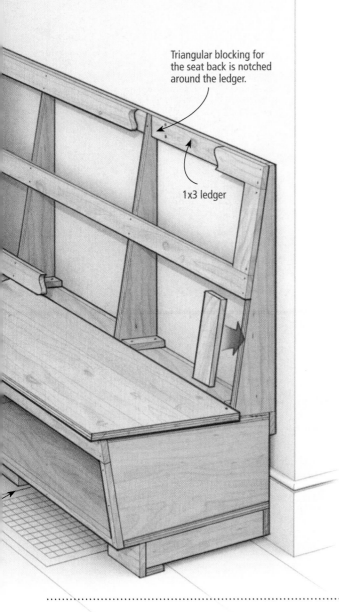

Triangular blocking for the seat back is notched around the ledger.

1x3 ledger

3 ASSEMBLE ELEMENTS OF THE BACK FRAME. On the right side, a 1x3 ledger screwed to the wall establishes the height of the back. Triangular pieces of plywood blocking are plumbed up and nailed to the base. Horizontal nailers then are attached across the top, middle, and bottom.

4 A LEDGER FOR THE WINDOW SHELF is nailed to the window apron. On the left, the triangular blocking is attached to the window casing and corner post; no ledger is needed.

5 TIE BOTH SIDES TOGETHER. The corner storage unit's face frame is extended across to the sides to provide blocking for the seat-back transition.

6 **INSTALL THE BEADBOARD FROM THE CORNER OUT.** Starting to the right of the bottom of the corner unit, nail the first board on a plumb line.

7 **FIND THE ANGLE.** The corner unit's beadboard intersects at a compound angle. From the edge of the face frame, measure top and bottom.

8 **FIT THE BOARD.** After cutting the compound angle with a saw guide, nail it against the first board. After repeating the process on the other side of the corner unit, fill in the rest of the boards out to the ends.

CAP THINGS OFF WITH SOLID PINE

The seat back and sides are covered with ¾-in. solid-pine beadboard milled in the shop. The area on each side of the window casing is filled in with the same stock. The plywood cap is scribed in place on the corner cabinet and butted to the solid-pine cap stock that runs along the back. Solid-pine nosings hide plywood edges.

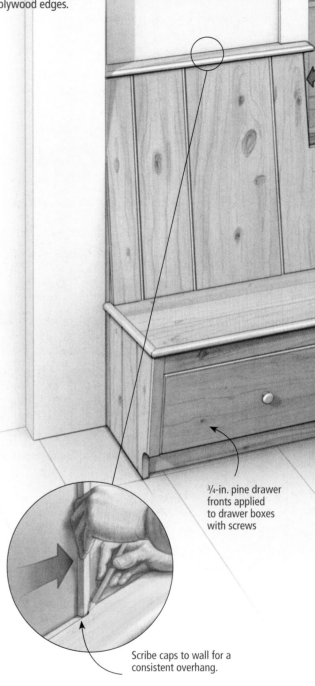

¾-in. pine drawer fronts applied to drawer boxes with screws

Scribe caps to wall for a consistent overhang.

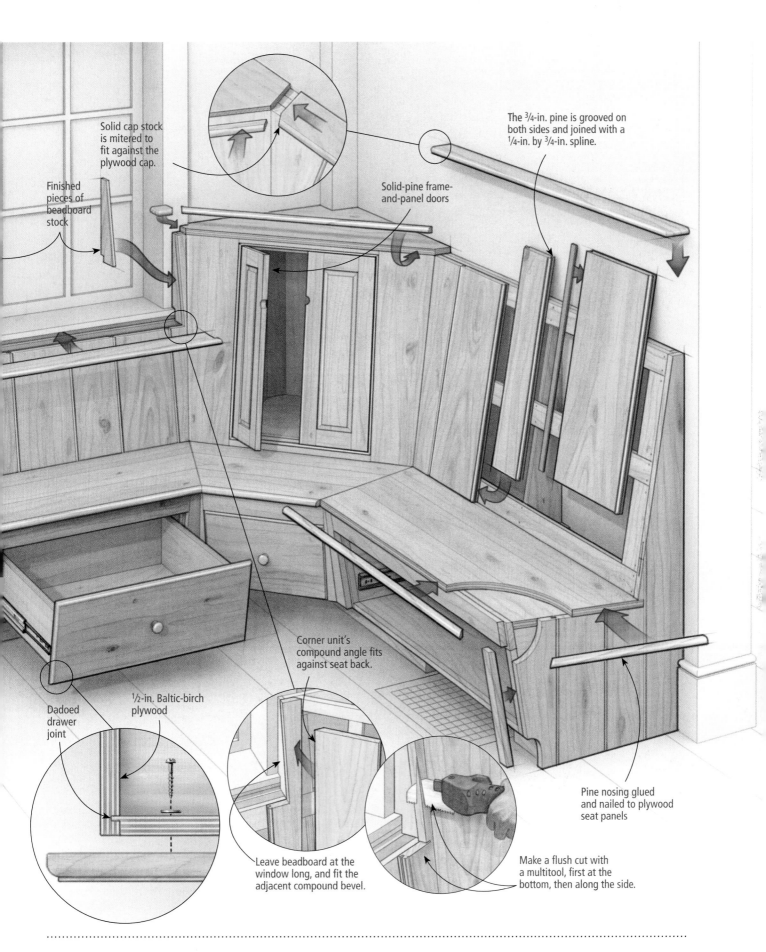

Solid cap stock is mitered to fit against the plywood cap.

Finished pieces of beadboard stock

The ¾-in. pine is grooved on both sides and joined with a ¼-in. by ¾-in. spline.

Solid-pine frame-and-panel doors

Corner unit's compound angle fits against seat back.

Dadoed drawer joint

½-in. Baltic-birch plywood

Leave beadboard at the window long, and fit the adjacent compound bevel.

Pine nosing glued and nailed to plywood seat panels

Make a flush cut with a multitool, first at the bottom, then along the side.

BATHROOMS & CLOSETS

Matching recessed medicine cabinets

Tall cabinets

12-in.-deep appliance garage with outlet inside

Tiered drawer divider

Door storage rack

U-shaped shelf

Tilt-out tray

Roll-out trays

Better Bathroom Storage

BY JAMIE GOLD ▮ The house I grew up in had only one full bathroom, which my parents, sister, brother, and I shared. Somehow, we made it work, as do millions of families today. But almost any bathroom will work better if a little more storage is added to the mix. The best time to maximize a

THREE WAYS TO BOOST BATHROOM STORAGE

1. INCREASE THE CAPACITY OF TRADITIONAL AREAS

- Add two-tiered organizers to any 4-in. or taller vanity drawer boxes, thus creating extra half-drawers without altering the existing cabinet.
- Install a storage rack on the back of every vanity base-cabinet door. Special racks are available for space-hogging hair dryers.
- Add roll-out trays to the bottom of base cabinets, and use them in place of shelves in linen towers, making what's stored in the back more visible and accessible.
- Wrap a U-shaped shelf around under-sink plumbing to add an extra level of storage.
- Convert the false panel below a vanity countertop to a tilt-out tray.

2. MAXIMIZE EXISTING FLOOR, SURFACE, AND WALL SPACE

- Maximize point-of-use vanity storage with countertop cabinetry. Use 12-in.-deep cabinets, keeping them at least 3 in. from the sink edge to prevent water damage. The cabinets can extend to the ceiling with a decorative crown molding, or stop a foot lower if there's a vent or light above. Regardless of height, they should be finished with a topcoat that protects against moisture, and be kept as dry as possible to prevent moisture damage at the point of contact with the vanity top.
- Increase point-of-use commode storage. If it is not situated under a window, install a single or stacked cabinet to the ceiling above the toilet. It should be low enough for a seated user to reach inside and extend no farther out than the toilet tank to avoid causing injury.
- If there is a window directly above the toilet, space might still exist for a shorter cabinet or shelf to be installed between the window and the ceiling for backup supplies. Ensure that the bottom is finished because it will be highly visible.
- Take advantage of unused floor space to create a built-in furniture armoire, floor cabinet, or storage bench for backup and occasional-use items. Remember to allow for clearances when adding storage of this type. National Kitchen & Bath Association design guidelines recommend 30 in. in front of a vanity, commode, or shower. NKBA guidelines are often more stringent than building codes, but be sure to check local requirements to ensure that you're in compliance whenever undertaking a bathroom project.

3. IDENTIFY STORAGE POSSIBILITIES IN NONTRADITIONAL SPACES

- Add a finished shelf above the bathroom entry door to take advantage of otherwise unused space for occasional-use items. Whenever possible, run it wall to wall.
- Take advantage of the forgotten space behind an in-swing door by building a tall, shallow cabinet into the wall between studs.
- Create a shower-wall niche for each bathroom occupant to accommodate daily point-of-use bathing items. At least one should be built within 15 in. of the shower bench for seated access.
- Plan open-storage cubbies for towels or bath supplies on the front end or exposed side of a new tub deck.
- Plan built-in, open wall-shelving units at one or both ends of a tub-only enclosure for daily point-of-use bathing items in storage baskets.

bathroom's storage capacity is, of course, at the design stage, but you can explore plenty of storage-boosting options while remodeling or simply when updating fixtures and cabinetry.

Whether incorporated into the original design or added after the fact, bathroom-storage expansion fits into three categories: (1) increasing the capacity of traditional storage areas like vanity cabinets; (2) maximizing existing floor and wall space with new storage options; and (3) identifying storage possibilities in spaces that are not traditionally used for storage. These approaches are outlined below, and strategies from all three are used in the illustrated examples.

Store it where you use it

The key to good bath storage begins by identifying all the items kept in the bathroom according to their point of use, which could be at the vanity, commode, tub, or shower. Items to be stored also fall into one of three use categories: daily, backup, and occasional.

Daily-use items like shampoo in the shower require space at their point of use. Backup items are extras of daily-use necessities, like the remaining five bars in the soap package. They need not clutter the point-of-use area; instead, they can be kept in their own storage space. Occasional-use items like cold medicine can be kept in the bathroom, where they'll probably be used, but they also can move outside the bathroom for storage.

Once a bathroom's storage needs are identified, solutions can be designed based on point-of-use and non-point-of-use opportunities.

The full-function vanity

It's not uncommon even for large vanity units to fall short on functional storage. In the example on p. 81, the space between the sinks is wider than 30 in., allowing a stacked 24-in.-wide butt-door cabinet pair. The double doors and lack of a center stile allow access from both sides. The lower unit is backless and contains a wall outlet, making it useful for housing and charging electric shavers and electric toothbrushes. The 12-in.-deep space above houses daily-use items that are too large for the medicine cabinets.

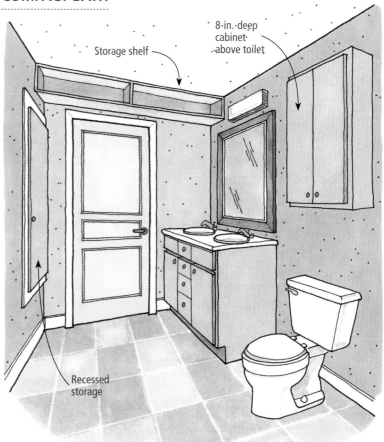

Storage shelf

8-in.-deep cabinet above toilet

Recessed storage

False panels in the sink bases have been converted to tilt-out trays for toothpaste and dental-floss storage. Doors are equipped with storage racks, including one for hair dryers. If extra storage is needed, U-shaped shelves can double the capacity of the sink cabinets. The center drawer's functionality is increased with a tiered divider, while the basic linen tower has been made more useful with a quartet of roll-out trays in the lower section.

The compact bath

This typical, small master bath offers occupants two sinks and a shared drawer bank but not much more in the way of storage. National Kitchen & Bath Association design guidelines recommend 30 in. of clearance (or a minimum of 21 in.) in front of the vanity and toilet, eliminating the opportunity for floor storage on the opposite wall. However, a 12-in.-deep shelf runs the length of the wall above the entry door to hold occasional-use items. The shelf can be supported by L-brackets or decorative supports, as long as they don't interfere with the door swing below. Taking advantage of otherwise unusable space behind the in-swing door is a tall, shallow cabinet installed between the wall studs. It holds occasional-use items that might otherwise be stored in a recessed medicine cabinet, freeing that valuable point-of-use space for daily needs. An 8-in.-deep cabinet above and within reach of the toilet offers point-of-use storage for spare rolls of tissue and other items.

The maximized master bath

The remodeled bath below maximizes daily point-of-use space in all three functional areas: tub, vanity, and toilet. The water closet features a floor cabinet for backup toilet paper, a toilet brush, and toilet-cleaning supplies. The wall cabinets above the toilet, only 8 in. deep to avoid collisions, hold supplies within reach of the user. Occasional-use items for the water closet can be stored in the upper section. The shower includes double niches to hold each occupant's bathing necessities. One is within 15 in. of the shower bench for easy reach. The tub deck is extended with storage in front for towels and other bath essentials. The deeper deck also facilitates a safer sit-and-swivel entry. In the vanity area, the linen tower offers space for a roll-out hamper in the bottom section. The opposite vanity takes advantage of an extrawide countertop to offer additional storage above for small electric devices with access to an outlet. Each wall cabinet is only 12 in. deep to allow counter space in front.

Jamie Gold, CKD, CAPS, is a Certified Kitchen Designer in San Diego and the author of *New Kitchen Ideas That Work* (The Taunton Press, 2012). You can find her designs and blog online at www.jgkitchens.com. Illustrations by Martha Garstang Hill.

MAXIMIZED MASTER

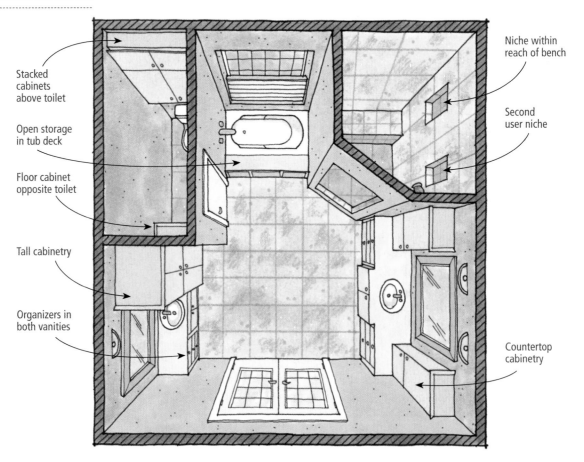

Stacked cabinets above toilet

Open storage in tub deck

Floor cabinet opposite toilet

Tall cabinetry

Organizers in both vanities

Niche within reach of bench

Second user niche

Countertop cabinetry

Build a Floating Vanity

BY NANCY R. HILLER As someone who prefers not to be vexed by job-related anxieties in the wee hours, I work hard to prevent foreseeable problems. On most jobs, gravity is the cabinetmaker's friend. When it comes to floating furniture, however, gravity poses certain challenges. If you don't take

CONT'D ON PAGE 88

PLYWOOD BOXES, BEAUTIFULLY DISGUISED

The vanity was made in three sections. The outer carcases are supported by brackets and angle irons. In turn, they support a center carcase that can be removed for permanent wheelchair access. Above the center carcase, a dummy panel conceals the sink.

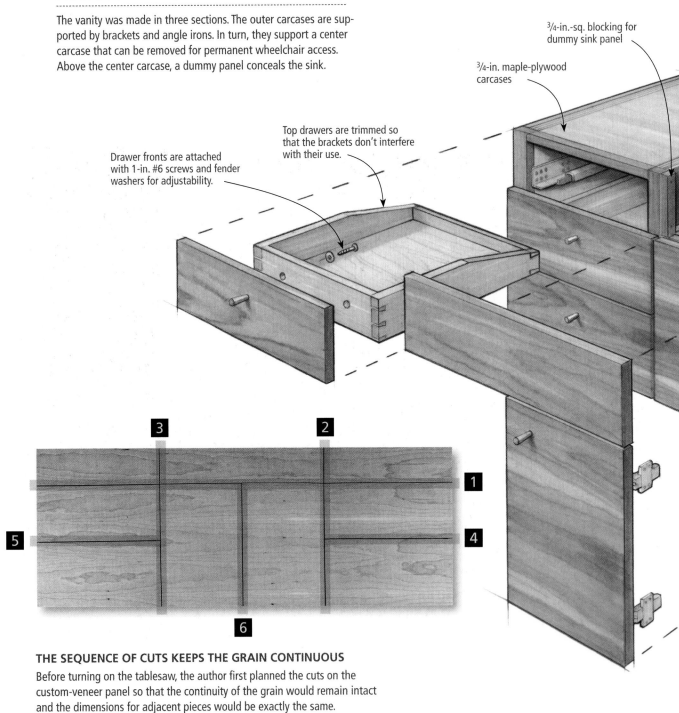

¾-in.-sq. blocking for dummy sink panel

¾-in. maple-plywood carcases

Top drawers are trimmed so that the brackets don't interfere with their use.

Drawer fronts are attached with 1-in. #6 screws and fender washers for adjustability.

THE SEQUENCE OF CUTS KEEPS THE GRAIN CONTINUOUS

Before turning on the tablesaw, the author first planned the cuts on the custom-veneer panel so that the continuity of the grain would remain intact and the dimensions for adjacent pieces would be exactly the same.

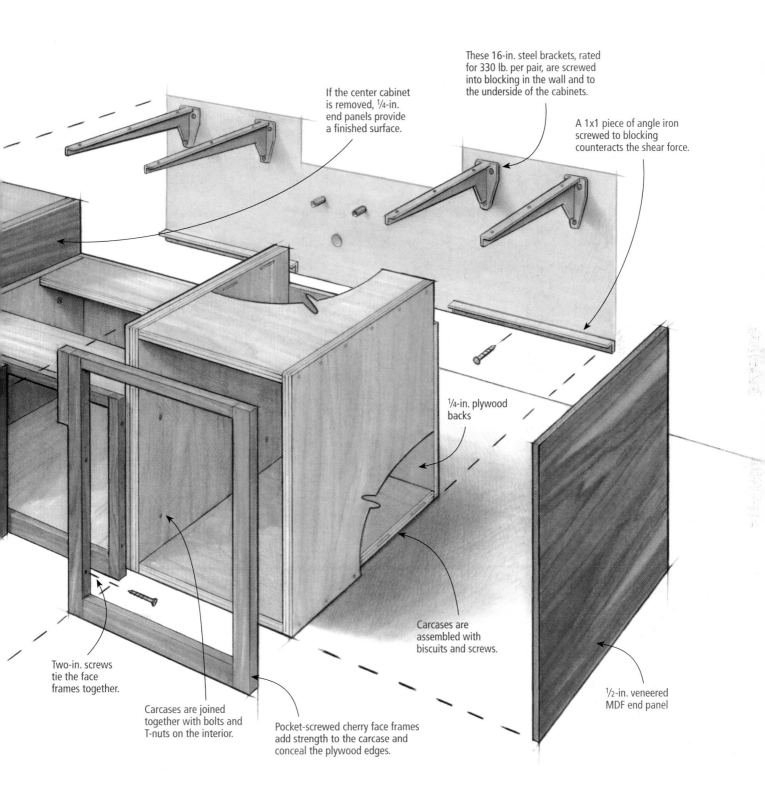

These 16-in. steel brackets, rated for 330 lb. per pair, are screwed into blocking in the wall and to the underside of the cabinets.

If the center cabinet is removed, ¼-in. end panels provide a finished surface.

A 1x1 piece of angle iron screwed to blocking counteracts the shear force.

¼-in. plywood backs

Carcases are assembled with biscuits and screws.

Two-in. screws tie the face frames together.

Carcases are joined together with bolts and T-nuts on the interior.

Pocket-screwed cherry face frames add strength to the carcase and conceal the plywood edges.

½-in. veneered MDF end panel

these challenges seriously, you may find yourself with a cabinet that wants to fall apart—or worse, one that falls off the wall.

Fine Homebuilding asked me to build a bathroom vanity for their Project House, and structural challenges were only one of the issues. Designed by architect Duncan McPherson, the cabinet's sleek, clean look depended on careful planning and on maintaining sharp lines. The vanity also was intended to be compliant with the Americans With Disabilities Act, so the center portion below the sink was to be removable for wheelchair access. To accentuate the horizontal shape, I wanted to wrap the exterior in the continuous grain of cherry-veneered moisture-resistant MDF; the carcases could be made from maple plywood. Solid maple drawers would be dovetailed for looks and strength.

Strength from fasteners and face frames

To build the cabinets, I began by cutting the case parts from prefinished ¾-in.-thick maple plywood. Because the sides of this cabinet were to have finished panels applied during installation, the ¼-in. plywood backs could simply be applied to the back of the cases, instead of housed in a groove or a rabbet.

To ensure the strength of these cabinets, I built them with biscuits interspersed with 2-in. Confirmat screws. After gluing and clamping the cases, I cleaned up glue squeeze-out and installed the screws.

Although the design is European-inspired, I added face frames to reinforce the structure of the cases and to have an alternative to veneer tape for covering the plywood edges.

Start with Strong Boxes

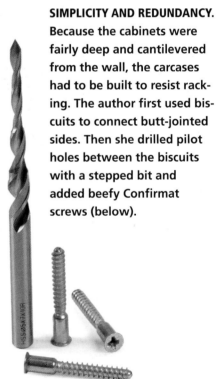

SIMPLICITY AND REDUNDANCY. Because the cabinets were fairly deep and cantilevered from the wall, the carcases had to be built to resist racking. The author first used biscuits to connect butt-jointed sides. Then she drilled pilot holes between the biscuits with a stepped bit and added beefy Confirmat screws (below).

I milled solid-cherry stiles and rails, and joined the parts with pocket screws to make the face frames. I attached each frame to its case with glue and clamps, positioning the clamps inside the box so that pressure would be applied at the visible joints between case edge and face frame. After cutting the ¼-in. backs for all three cases, I test-fit the cases to each other in their final configuration, using T-nuts, bolts, and screws to attach the removable center case to the outer sections.

Dovetailed drawers are easy with the right jig

Once the cases were fitted with their face frames, I installed the drawer slides. This way, I knew the exact dimensions of the drawer boxes. I also kept the hardware in mind when determining where to cut the groove for

drawer bottoms, because some types of drawer slides require a specific location relative to the bottom of the drawer side.

After cutting out the drawer parts from solid maple, I sanded the interior faces and set up the dovetail jig. Dovetails make a strong, beautiful drawer, but there was no reason for me to cut them by hand. Using a Keller jig (sidebar, p. 90), I can cut the four parts for one drawer in about 10 minutes. I cut the grooves for the ¼-in. plywood bottoms on the tablesaw and ripped the drawer back at the groove so that I could insert the bottom into the groove after the sides were assembled. Once the drawers were glued and clamped, I made sure that they were square and flat. I sanded the drawer boxes when the glue was dry, then inserted the drawer bottoms and fixed them in place with two small screws.

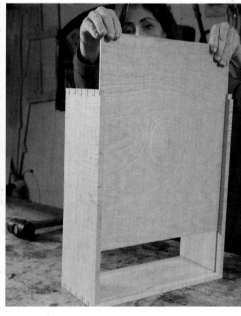

CLAMPING UP SQUARE. At this point in the assembly, the carcases don't have backs or anything else that will keep the four sides square until the glue dries. As I clamp together each carcase, I measure the diagonals (above). If the diagonals aren't equal, I offset the clamps on one side (right) until the box is square.

BOTTOM SLIDES IN LAST. After the glue had dried and the drawer assembly was square and flat, the author slid the plywood bottom into its groove (above) and fastened it with small screws to the underside of the back.

TEMPLATES FOR PRECISION

When I'm making cabinets, I'm in a production mind-set, so I use a router and a jig to cut the drawer dovetails. I've used several jigs, but the Keller jig is my favorite. It's incredibly simple and efficient, and it produces beautiful joints. The jig consists of two aluminum templates, one for the pins and one for the tails, that are clamped to the respective pieces. The set comes with top bearing-guided router bits.

Doors and drawer fronts from custom-veneer material

I could have bought a sheet of ¾-in. cherry plywood off the shelf to create the vanity front, but including the end panels meant that I'd need more than one sheet, and then the grain wouldn't be continuous. Luckily, there's a custom-veneer place in town where I was able to choose the veneer and how it would be laid up on three separate panels (sidebar, p. 92).

I marked out the door and drawer faces on the plywood so that the grain alignment would be continuous across the face of the cabinet. I cut the drawer fronts and doors, then edge-banded them with heat-sensitive veneer tape and sanded the tape flush at the edges. I also drilled holes and mounted the European hinges on the doors. After locating the hinge plates on the inside faces of the center cabinet by holding the doors in position and placing marks directly on the inside of the case, I put the doors aside until the cabinet installation.

Finish for a wet area

Bathroom cabinets should have a water-resistant finish. If I were building more cabinets, I would have them sprayed with a conversion varnish; for this one cabinet, though, I brushed on several coats of oil-based polyurethane. To prepare the cabinet parts for the polyurethane, I vacuumed, then wiped it all down with a tack rag moistened with mineral spirits to remove any remaining dust.

After brushing on a coat of polyurethane, I let it dry thoroughly overnight. The next day, I scuffed up the surfaces with 220-grit sandpaper, tacked again, and applied a second coat. I repeated the whole thing for a third coat, too.

Dial in a Precise Fit

THE BEST WAY TO MAKE IT FIT. To scribe each end panel to the wall, the author clamped the panel flush to the outside of the ¾-in. face frame, then used a ¾-in. scrap to mark the wall's contour.

CUSTOM VENEER IS A GAME CHANGER

I consider myself lucky to live in Bloomington, Ind., because there's a world-class custom-veneer shop right in town. Although Heitink Architectural Veneer and Plywood supplies more than 120 species of veneered products to architectural millwork clients for enormous commercial projects (Las Vegas casinos, for example), it also makes small projects like this one possible. Pallets of veneer come into the factory and are trimmed, glued, and spliced into sheets. The sheets then are laminated to substrates of any size or type. Heitink can arrange the panels' grain patterns to match sequentially so that an entire room can be wrapped in a unique pattern of wood grain.

NOTHING GETS BY THE INSPECTOR. After the veneer sheets are glued up, each is checked on a big light table for cracks, imperfections, and other hidden defects.

Dial in a Precise Fit, cont'd

MEASURE WITH COMMON CENTS. It's critical to maintain consistent spacing between drawer fronts, so rather than use a shim, the author used a pair of pennies between the faces to set the gap.

Putting it in place

Once on site, I began the installation by placing 2x blocking between the studs in the wall. Usually, you have to remove drywall to access the stud bays, but if you're careful, you can hide repairs behind the cabinet. (On this project, I had access to the back of the tiled wall.) Using heavy construction screws, I attached one line of blocking to support brackets for the top of the cabinet and another line below for angle iron at the base.

Next, I found the centerline of the wall and marked a horizontal line for the top of the casework. I located the tops of the upper brackets by measuring down ¾ in. from the line. Each outside cabinet would be supported by two brackets positioned as close as possible toward the sides of each case to avoid taking up space that could otherwise be used for storage inside the drawer. I marked and drilled the positions of the holes, then installed the brackets and checked across all four to confirm that they were level.

I set the outer cabinets on the brackets and transferred the measurements for the plumbing onto the back of the center cabinet. After cutting the holes and checking the fit, I installed the center cabinet by carefully lowering it

into place onto temporary supports. I then attached all three cases together by inserting bolts into the T-nuts. I screwed the outer cases onto the brackets and locked them into place. To draw the face frames tight, I also ran bolts through the face-frame edges.

I scribed the end panels to the wall and attached them with wood glue and brads. (The interior finished panels next to the center cabinet were cut and installed in the shop.) Now I was ready to finish the puzzle. I hung the doors, then attached each drawer face to its box with 1-in. #6 pan-head screws fitted through ¾-in. by ⅛-in. fender washers. I carefully adjusted the faces until they were even across the entire assembly. (Placing coins between the faces is a great way to maintain even margins between the elements.) Finally, I fit the central dummy panel that will conceal the sink and attached it to the outside cases by screwing it to the blocks above the center cabinet.

Nancy R. Hiller (www.nrhillerdesign.com) is a professional maker of custom furniture and cabinetry based in Bloomington, Ind. She specializes in period-authentic furniture and built-ins for homes and offices from the late-19th through mid-20th centuries. Illustrations by Bob La Pointe.

IN A PERFECT WORLD, SCREWS WOULD BE ENOUGH

I calculated that the cabinet would weigh 207 lb. Add to this the concrete counter (which will sometimes be holding a full sink of water), the cabinet's contents, and the likelihood that someone, someday, will think that it makes sense to stand on the cabinet while changing a lightbulb, and the total load could exceed 350 lb. For this job, I decided to use brackets rated for 330 lb. per pair, which I found at Häfele, the cabinet-hardware supply company. To counteract the shear, I bought 1-in. by 1-in. steel angle iron from my local welding shop. After cutting it to the width of each side cabinet, I drilled holes into one side and screwed the pieces to the wall, against the underside of the cabinet.

A Master-Suite Closet

BY PAUL DEGROOT ■
A master suite is typically a top priority for architect Paul DeGroot's clients. Here are some of his tips for creating a master-suite closet that is big on function regardless of its size or configuration.

Don't be stingy

Closets are the workhorse of the master suite. Although you need only 16 sq. ft. (with a 24-in.-wide door) for a walk-in closet, don't stop there. Provide as much closet space as you can possibly squeeze in. If one large closet won't work, find room for two smaller closets. Determine how many linear feet of clothes rod are needed. Whenever you can, use double rods—one high, one low. Eliminate the lower rod where long coats and dresses will hang.

START WITH THE BASICS. In a walk-in closet, the must-haves include dresser drawers, open shelves, counter space, and hanging rods. You can fit two hanging rods for shirts and jackets on most walls. For longer items, one higher rod is necessary. A tubular skylight illuminates this walk-in closet even on overcast days, and a door does double-duty concealing shoe storage and as a full-length mirror (facing page).

FUNCTION FROM FLOOR TO CEILING.
In this closet, additional shelves
placed above clothing rods provide
storage space for infrequently
used items, such as luggage.

Avoid exterior walls

The bedroom and the bathroom can better use the space for windows and doors. Exceptions include using a closet as a thermal buffer from a hot west-facing wall (or a cold north wall) or placing a closet along a wall that faces the street or a neighbor's house.

Make room to reach in

Reach-in-closet openings should be wide enough so that reaching beyond the door jamb is easy. If you have space for a 7-ft.-long reach-in closet, you should plan on a minimum 5-ft. door width.

Consider lighting

If you're stuck with an exterior wall for your walk-in closet, you might choose to include small windows so that you don't always need to hit the light switch. But make sure to keep direct sun from fading clothes. Tubular skylights are a great alternative to windows.

Leave room to dress

A walk-in closet with clothes hanging on both walls should be at least 7 ft. wide, which nets a 36-in. center walkway. If the closet is big enough to be used as a dressing area, make room for a chair or a stool and a full-length mirror.

DIRTY CLOTHES NEED A PLACE TO GO. A hamper is easy to incorporate into the lower portion of a cabinet in the closet or bath. In place of a drawer, a fold-down door accepts dirty clothes that fall into a basket in the cabinet below.

Use pocket doors

Pocket doors are perfect for walk-in closets because they save space and stay open most of the time. There is excellent hardware available; for heavy doors, insist on top-quality ball-bearing rollers and the best track available.

Add function with accessories

Whether you choose store-bought, wall-mounted closet systems or custom built-ins, go for the accessories. I often call for two built-in dressers to hold folded clothes. Each has a countertop above the drawers with a handy outlet for charging a cell phone. Above that are adjustable shelves. Racks of adjustable shelves for shoes are always appreciated, as are deep shelves for luggage. Where ceilings are 9 ft. or higher, I specify an extra shelf 12 in. to 15 in. below the ceiling for long-term storage.

Paul DeGroot (www.degrootarchitect.com) is an architect who designs custom homes and additions in Austin, Texas.

SIMPLE SHOE STORAGE. A typical shelf design can be easily transformed into useful shoe storage by offsetting the shelf pins and turning the shelves upside down. The nosing extends to keep shoes from sliding off the tilted shelf.

STANLEY

MUDROOMS

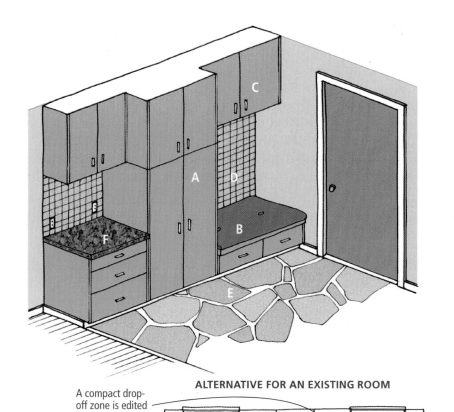

THE DROP-OFF ZONE

A. A coat cabinet is more space efficient than a coat closet. It helps to keep the drop-off zone compact.

B. An 18-in.-high bench that accommodates at least one person provides a spot for putting on and taking off shoes.

C. Door and drawer fronts with high-quality pulls help to make the zone more formal.

D. Wainscot or tiles provide a level of protection and adornment fit for the main entrance and living space.

E. High-quality, resilient flooring such as stone is durable and should be used to distinguish the zone from adjacent living spaces.

F. A staging area provides a spot to rest groceries, bags, and packages while you transition from outside to inside.

ALTERNATIVE FOR AN EXISTING ROOM

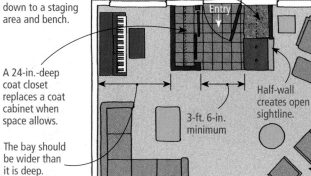

A compact drop-off zone is edited down to a staging area and bench.

A 24-in.-deep coat closet replaces a coat cabinet when space allows.

The bay should be wider than it is deep.

Entry

3-ft. 6-in. minimum

Half-wall creates open sightline.

Intimate bays on each side of the front door are created through the construction of new entry walls.

Transitional Entries

BY LAURA KRAFT ▮ Design that acknowledges daily transitions from private lives to the public world beyond our doors adds to the quality of life within a home. In more practical terms, having a place to exchange slippers for street shoes, or vice versa, makes a home a more functional, comfortable place to live.

These transitional areas are called drop-off zones when they're at the entry, and mudrooms when they're next to the garage or at the back of the house. In a recent American Institute of Architects' survey of housing trends, homeowners have indicated increasing interest in both spaces.

The demands placed on these spaces differ relative to their location in the home. The users' needs determine the elements to be included, and the home's architectural style and layout affect how the elements are designed.

Here, I've highlighted a few of the most important details worth considering when designing these spaces. I've also shared examples of how these spaces can be adapted to fit two common floor plans.

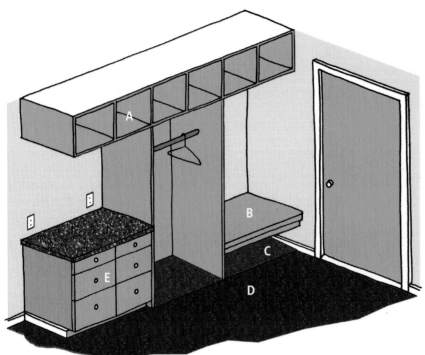

THE MUDROOM

A. Open cubbies provide quick access to stowed items such as hats, gloves, or sporting equipment.

B. An easy-to-clean bench provides a spot to sit and change footwear.

C. The floor below the bench and in the bottom of the closet slopes to accommodate wet shoes and boots.

D. Resilient flooring such as Marmoleum® withstands the rigors of a high-traffic zone.

E. Drawers with workhorse-grade pulls are tailored to daily household usage.

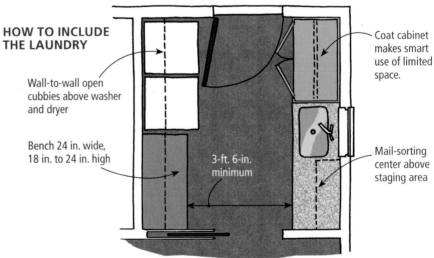

HOW TO INCLUDE THE LAUNDRY

Wall-to-wall open cubbies above washer and dryer

Bench 24 in. wide, 18 in. to 24 in. high

3-ft. 6-in. minimum

Coat cabinet makes smart use of limited space.

Mail-sorting center above staging area

The front of the house: the drop-off zone

In the past I emphasized the drop-off zone as a focal point for charging and storing electronic gadgets. As the nature of gadgets has evolved from single-function gizmos into responsive, multifunction, sleek beauties, people have become more attached to them. I now find that most people charge their phones and tablets close to where they work, eat, or sleep—not in the drop-off zone. While I still provide a couple of electrical receptacles for my clients, I have refined the designs of these spaces.

What hasn't changed is the near-universal dislike among my clients with older houses of front doors opening directly into the living room (bottom drawing, p. 99). They want to have a transitional space, and most are willing to trade a few square feet of living room for it.

The back of the house: the mudroom

The difference between a drop-off zone and a mudroom lies in the subtle details of their design and the rugged material choices used in their construction. A mudroom should be thought of as a utilitarian space, fit to take the heavy use of a busy household. In many cases, the mudroom is adjacent to the family's primary entrance, such as a back door accessed from a garage, carport, or yard. Adjust the design of this space by carefully considering the items you bring through this entrance. For instance, if the mudroom is close to the kitchen, increase the size of the staging area to hold more groceries. If it's near the backyard garden, include cubbies for garden supplies and work wear. Although a mudroom lacks the formality of a front-of-home drop-off zone, it plays no less a role in the organization of your living space.

The mail center add-on

Depending on the location of your mailbox and the entrance you use most often to access it, a mail-sorting center could be integrated into your drop-off zone or mudroom. In any mail-sorting center, it is wise to locate recycling and trash bins within arm's reach of the cubbies and countertop. A built-in like this keeps junk mail and clutter from making their way into primary living spaces.

Laura Kraft (lkarchitect.com) is an architect in Seattle. Drawings by the author.

THE MAIL CENTER

A. Cubbies should be a minimum of 4 in. wide.

B. Cubbies 12 in. tall by 12 in. deep are most accommodating.

C. Scale the pullout to the size of the recycling and trash bins.

D. Larger cubbies provide storage for incoming and outgoing packages as well as often-used items such as dog leashes, hats, and gloves.

Outfit a Mudroom with Functional Storage

BY GARY STRIEGLER ▪ Even if you live in a place where it's 80°F and sunny all the time, you probably still need a mudroom. It's like an air lock in a spaceship, a transition area between the outside and the inside. A well-designed mudroom should have space to store coats, backpacks, boots, and everything else that family members use on a daily basis. It also should be a comfortable place where you can complete the last steps of dressing before facing the outside world.

Mudrooms are usually shared spaces, but when I build them, I like to provide some personal storage space for each family member— and still keep it out in the open. After all, it's a lot harder to forget something when it's right in front of you. I also think it's important to have some concealed storage for things such as umbrellas that you don't need every day. When shelving is part of my storage design, I make it adjustable. There is no telling what you'll need to store down the road. Finally, I want every mudroom to have some counter space for things like cell phones, keys, and books.

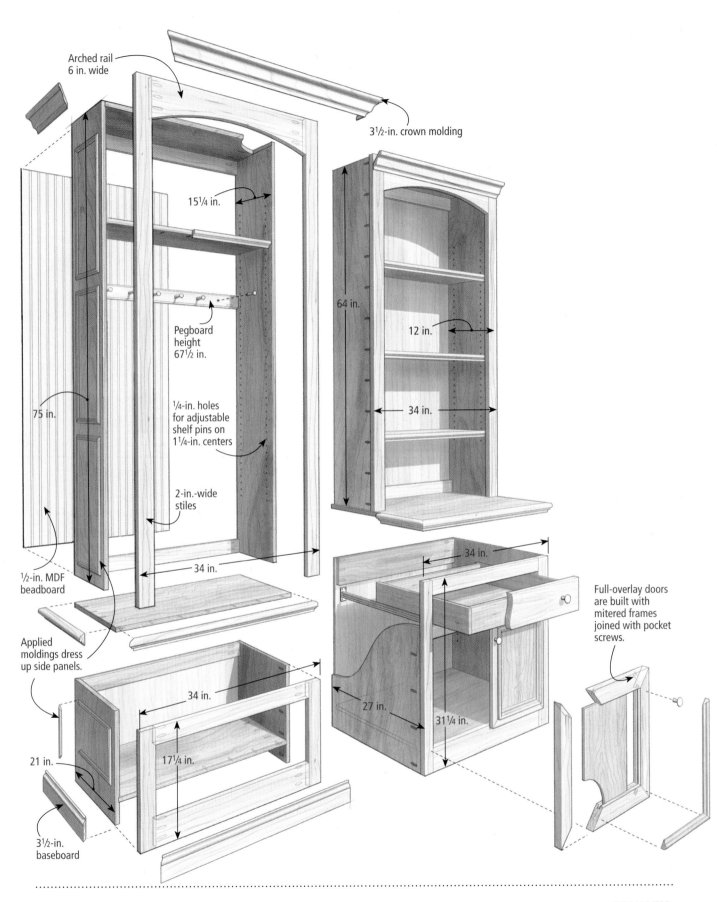

Arched rail 6 in. wide

3½-in. crown molding

15¼ in.

Pegboard height 67½ in.

¼-in. holes for adjustable shelf pins on 1¼-in. centers

2-in.-wide stiles

75 in.

½-in. MDF beadboard

Applied moldings dress up side panels.

34 in.

64 in.

12 in.

34 in.

Full-overlay doors are built with mitered frames joined with pocket screws.

34 in.

27 in.

31¼ in.

21 in.

34 in.

17¼ in.

3½-in. baseboard

Built in the shop, on site

When I build a cabinet on site, I use the same basic methods that I would use in a shop. I build the cabinet boxes, attach face frames, then screw the boxes to the wall and to each other. To do this, I employ a few special tools to create a mini-shop. My track saw lets me cut sheet goods in a fairly tight space, and because the saw moves instead of the plywood, it's a one-man job. When cutting sheet goods with a tablesaw, I need a total of 20 ft. of space. With a track saw, I need about 10 ft. The only drawback is that I have to measure and mark each piece when I'm making multiple cuts.

When I'm building cabinet boxes, accuracy and strength are important. Kreg Tool Company's Foreman makes fast work of drilling the pocket holes I use for joining cases and face frames. Unlike the company's pocket-screw jig, this machine is self-contained and drills pilot holes with a lever-actuated indexing mechanism. The screws give me a strong joint without a lot of nail holes on the sides of the cabinet, and they pull the joints tight without clamps. Pocket-screw joints are more efficient than biscuit joints because you machine only one of the two pieces being joined. There are no problems with alignment and there's no clamp time. As soon as the screw is driven, I can move to the next step.

My miter saw sits in a homemade stand that has wide outfeed surfaces and a built-in clamp to hold my work if I need to use the stand as a secondary workbench. Most important, it has an adjustable-stop system so that I can make accurate repetitive cuts of face-frame and door parts.

CONT'D ON PAGE 108 ▶

A DEDICATED SPACE FOR EVERYONE

1. Coats can be hung from pegs. The cabinet sides are drilled for adjustable shelves, and they can be fitted with a closet pole.
2. Adjustable shelves offer space for items used less often. The shelves also can be used to display objects.
3. At 32 in. high, the counter is a convenient place for dropping briefcases, books, keys, and cell phones.
4. Below, a drawer and a pair of doors provide concealed storage.
5. An 18-in.-high seat makes a convenient place to change shoes. Shoe and boot storage is directly below.

Join with Pocket Screws and Dadoes

1 MAKE THE CUT. First, cut plywood parts to size with a track saw.

2 CUT THE DADOES. With a straight router bit and fence, cut 1/8-in. by 3/4-in. dadoes in the cabinet side to house the top and bottom pieces, followed by 3/4-in. by 1/2-in. dadoes on each piece to receive the plywood back.

3 DRILL FOR FLEXIBLE STORAGE. Drill the holes for the adjustable shelf pins. The author uses a store-bought jig.

4 THEN DRILL THE POCKET HOLES. Drill the pocket holes used for joining the cases and the face frames (inset).

5 PUT IT ALL TOGETHER. Assemble the boxes by clamping the pieces together and securing them with screws.

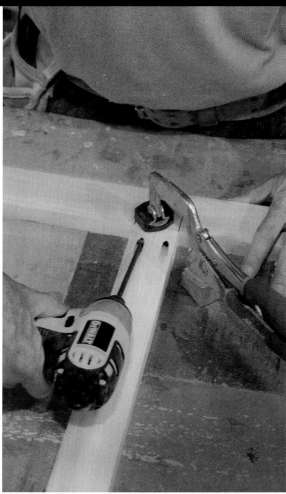

SAVE TIME WITH POCKET SCREWS. Gluing and clamping face frames to cabinets takes time. Attaching face frames with nails creates holes that must be filled. Pocket screws don't require long clamping time, and they create a fast and positive joint both for assembling and attaching the face frames.

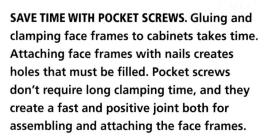

CONCEAL THE SCREWS. Face-frame joints are typically concealed (top right), but in certain situations (bottom right), visible holes can be filled with Kreg's proprietary dowel plugs (bottom far right).

Most cabinet shops are set up around a large tablesaw and a heavy-duty planer. Because all my lumber is surfaced before it comes to the job site, I need only a portable planer to remove sawkerfs from the edges of the lumber after it is ripped. (Always remember to rip pieces about 1/8 in. wider than you need so that the edges can be cleaned up.) A small tablesaw will do everything that I need done on the job site as long as I pair it with a good outfeed table that doubles as my main workbench.

Installing square boxes in an unsquare world

The installation process marries the measured geometry of the boxes to the often irregular condition of the room. If you are setting upper and lower cabinets separated by a backsplash, it's almost always easier to set the uppers first. However, in this mudroom, the uppers sit on base cabinets that must be installed first. I always start base-cabinet installation by checking the floor for level. I prefer to set cabinets at the highest corner and then shim everything

Install from the Ground Up

A LEVEL BASE IS ESSENTIAL. Base cabinets are installed first and should be shimmed level. Marking the location of framing in the wall makes it easier to screw cabinets to the studs.

1 TAKE THE WALL CONDITION INTO ACCOUNT. Any hollows in the wall should be shimmed out to prevent distortion of the cabinet backs when the screws are tightened.

STANLEY

else up to that point. If I can't start at the highest point, I carry the high point around the room and shim the first cabinet up to it. If the finished floor hasn't been installed, I add shims so that there are no problems when installing appliances after the floor is down.

It's also a good idea to check walls for plumb and to use a straightedge to check for humps. Bows or dips across the face of the wall will wreck a nice straight line of upper cabinets, so the cabinets may have to be shimmed out to keep the front edge straight.

When I cut the backs of cabinets for wiring or electrical boxes, I work from the side that will give the cleanest cut on the visible side. I also make allowances for out-of-plumb walls and factor in the amount the face-frame hangs beyond the sides of the plywood box. Remember, too, that a pilot hole is a great idea if you're screwing face frames together.

Gary Striegler, a frequent contributor to Fine Homebuilding, *is a custom-home builder in Fayetteville, Ark. He teaches each summer at the Marc Adams School of Woodworking and works with Mercy International on building projects in Honduras. Illustration by John Hartman.*

2 **ADD THE UPPER CABINET.** The first upper cabinet is placed on the base. Note that the base counter is attached to the upper cabinet first so that the exposed joint is as tight as possible. Trim screws join the two cabinets to each other and to the framing.

3 **CONCEAL YOUR SCREWS.** Whenever possible, locate screws behind face frames or other less visible spots. Clamps provide a third hand to keep the joint tight between two cabinets while driving in screws.

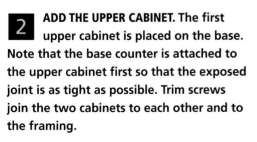

4 **ADD THE FINISHING TOUCHES.** After the boxes have been assembled, the crown molding, baseboard, and other trim can be installed.

A Stylish Mudroom Built-in

BY TONY O'MALLEY An enclosed porch or mudroom can help keep dirt and snow from reaching the living areas of your house. It's also a great place to stow stuff you'd rather not have cluttering the kitchen or family room: boots, shoes, book bags, sports gear, and the like. But without designated storage areas, a mudroom becomes a minefield. An elegant solution is to make a built-in storage cabinet, which will not only look good and organize your life, but can also add value to your home.

This mudroom unit features a base cabinet topped with open locker-type cabinets. The base cabinet has a lift-lid section for stowing out-of-season stuff like winter boots. The upper cabinets have fixed shelves and hooks for jackets. This piece is designed for a family of four—with each person getting his or her own locker space—but it can easily be made larger or smaller to suit a different-size family.

The construction is simple: maple plywood cases with walnut face frames and applied frame-and-panel assemblies, which give the piece a furniture feel. Most of the parts are made in the shop and assembled on site.

Build the plywood boxes first

For this project, I used prefinished ¾-in.-thick maple plywood for all the cases. Though not commonly available at major home centers, the plywood often can be special-

ordered at lumberyards. It saves you considerable finishing time, and creates a bright, durable interior that looks great with the dark walnut exterior.

For the upper lockers, I made four identical skinny cabinets and screwed them together. These smaller cabinets are easier to build, move around in the shop, and install. And this method can make the difference between needing a helper and getting the job done on your own. The plywood edges on the upper lockers are hidden with solid-walnut face frames, which are glued and nailed in place. To help align the face frames, I used ⅛-in.-thick splines cut from tempered Masonite. Before assembling the cases, I cut the grooves for the splines in all the front edges using a router and a slot-cutting bit. To assemble the cases, I used screws and biscuits.

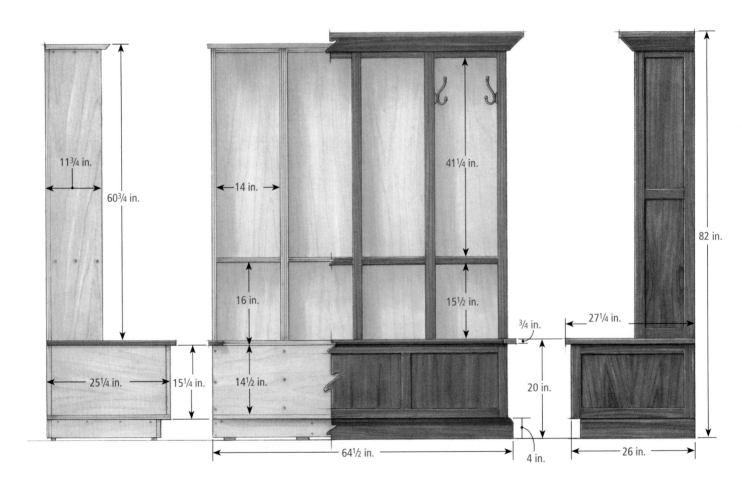

BASE CABINET OFFERS SEATING AND STORAGE

The lower cabinet is a plywood box faced with walnut frames and panels. The height is perfect for sitting to change shoes, and the lidded box has plenty of room for items you don't want to see, like boots and outdoor gear.

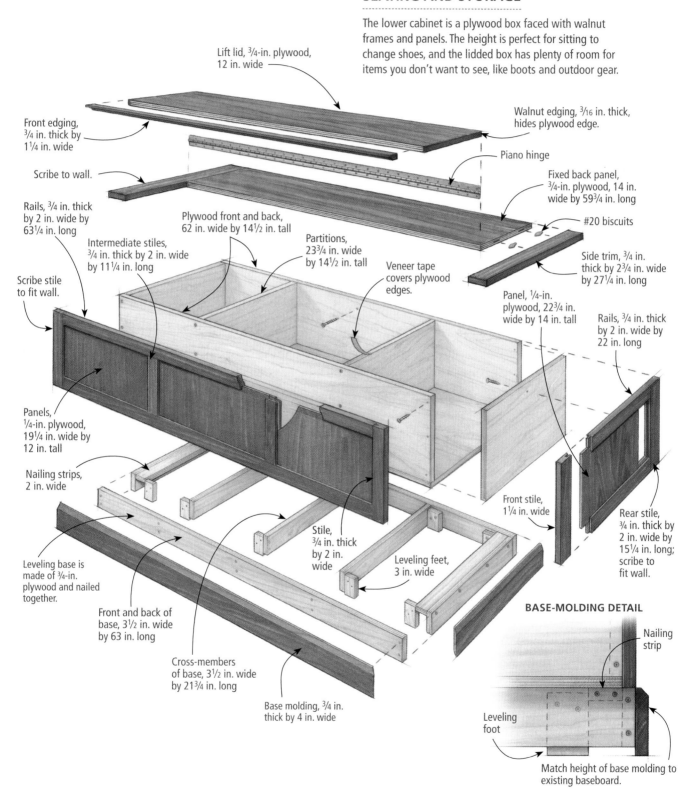

Lift lid, ³/₄-in. plywood, 12 in. wide

Front edging, ³/₄ in. thick by 1¹/₄ in. wide

Walnut edging, ³/₁₆ in. thick, hides plywood edge.

Scribe to wall.

Piano hinge

Fixed back panel, ³/₄-in. plywood, 14 in. wide by 59³/₄ in. long

Rails, ³/₄ in. thick by 2 in. wide by 63¹/₄ in. long

Plywood front and back, 62 in. wide by 14¹/₂ in. tall

Partitions, 23³/₄ in. wide by 14¹/₂ in. tall

#20 biscuits

Intermediate stiles, ³/₄ in. thick by 2 in. wide by 11¹/₄ in. long

Veneer tape covers plywood edges.

Side trim, ³/₄ in. thick by 2³/₄ in. wide by 27¹/₄ in. long

Scribe stile to fit wall.

Panel, ¹/₄-in. plywood, 22³/₄ in. wide by 14 in. tall

Rails, ³/₄ in. thick by 2 in. wide by 22 in. long

Panels, ¹/₄-in. plywood, 19¹/₄ in. wide by 12 in. tall

Nailing strips, 2 in. wide

Front stile, 1¹/₄ in. wide

Rear stile, ³/₄ in. thick by 2 in. wide by 15¹/₄ in. long; scribe to fit wall.

Leveling base is made of ³/₄-in. plywood and nailed together.

Stile, ³/₄ in. thick by 2 in. wide

Leveling feet, 3 in. wide

Front and back of base, 3¹/₂ in. wide by 63 in. long

Cross-members of base, 3¹/₂ in. wide by 21³/₄ in. long

Base molding, ³/₄ in. thick by 4 in. wide

BASE-MOLDING DETAIL

Nailing strip

Leveling foot

Match height of base molding to existing baseboard.

UPPER CABINETS SERVE AS LOCKERS

The top cabinets are individual plywood boxes screwed together and faced with solid walnut. These lockers have small cubbies for backpacks, purses, and briefcases, and larger spaces to hang coats and jackets.

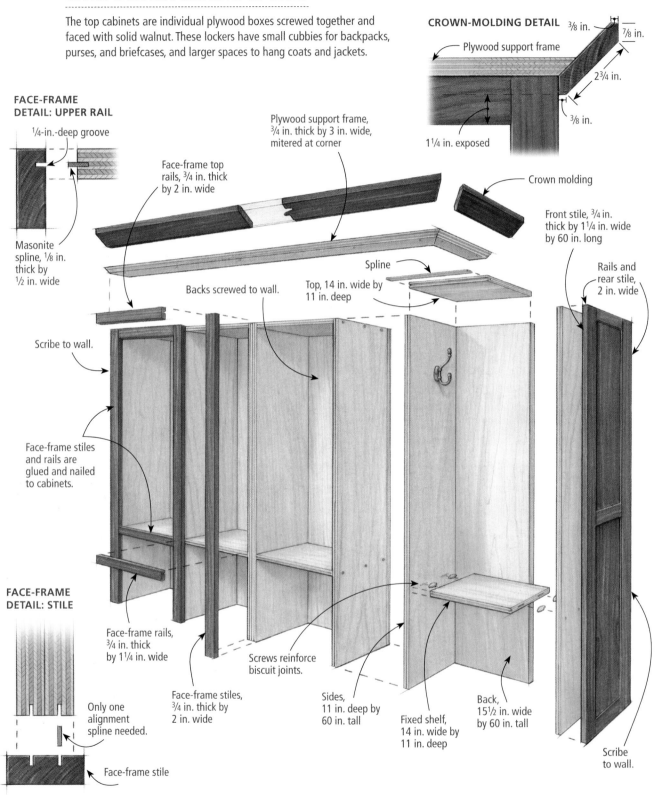

CROWN-MOLDING DETAIL

Plywood support frame

3/8 in.

7/8 in.

2 3/4 in.

3/8 in.

1 1/4 in. exposed

FACE-FRAME DETAIL: UPPER RAIL

1/4-in.-deep groove

Masonite spline, 1/8 in. thick by 1/2 in. wide

Face-frame top rails, 3/4 in. thick by 2 in. wide

Plywood support frame, 3/4 in. thick by 3 in. wide, mitered at corner

Crown molding

Front stile, 3/4 in. thick by 1 1/4 in. wide by 60 in. long

Rails and rear stile, 2 in. wide

Spline

Top, 14 in. wide by 11 in. deep

Backs screwed to wall.

Scribe to wall.

Face-frame stiles and rails are glued and nailed to cabinets.

FACE-FRAME DETAIL: STILE

Only one alignment spline needed.

Face-frame stile

Face-frame rails, 3/4 in. thick by 1 1/4 in. wide

Face-frame stiles, 3/4 in. thick by 2 in. wide

Screws reinforce biscuit joints.

Sides, 11 in. deep by 60 in. tall

Fixed shelf, 14 in. wide by 11 in. deep

Back, 15 1/2 in. wide by 60 in. tall

Scribe to wall.

Base cabinet is built the same way

The base cabinet for this built-in goes together with the same biscuit and screw joinery as the locker cabinets. One difference is that I used an adhesive-backed maple edge-banding on the top edge of the two exposed partitions.

Put on the edge-banding before you cut the partitions to size. That way, the banded partitions don't vary in size from the unbanded ends of the case. Trim the edge-banding with a chisel.

Make and prefinish the walnut parts

Once the plywood cases are glued up, you can begin working on the walnut face frames, the frame-and-panel

Clean Cuts in Plywood

RIP, THEN CROSSCUT. When breaking down a full sheet of plywood on a tablesaw, rip the pieces to size, then crosscut them using a sled.

THE FINAL CUTS. To reduce tearout, keep the show face on top, and use a good combination blade and a zero-clearance insert or crosscut sled. To further reduce the chances of tearout during a crosscut, apply masking tape over the bottom side of the cut line.

Biscuits and Screws Speed Assembly

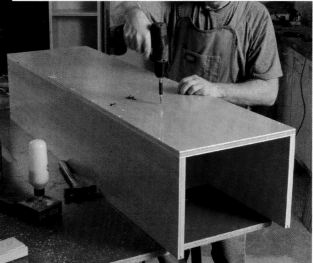

NO CLAMPS REQUIRED. Assemble the shelves, top, and sides with biscuits and screws. The screws not only reinforce the biscuits, but they also eliminate the need for clamps. Drill clearance holes and countersinks in the top pieces, and pilot holes in the edges below to prevent splitting.

assemblies, and the lift-lid assembly. All of the walnut parts should be finished (I used Minwax® Wipe-On Poly) before installation. It's much easier that way.

Because most walls aren't square or flat, you'll need to fit the end pieces of the built-in to that irregular surface. So leave any piece that butts against the wall about 3/8 in. oversize in width (or length for the moldings) to allow for scribing and fitting.

Face frame

Mill the face-frame stock to thickness and width, but leave the pieces long. They'll be trimmed to fit the case during installation. That will leave the end grain unfinished, but no one will see it. I chamfer the edges and ends of every face-frame part to create a small V-groove at each intersection; this detail not only looks good but

Lift Lid: A Lesson in Edging Plywood

FIXED BACK GETS SOLID EDGES. Attach the side trim pieces to the fixed back with biscuits.

HIDE EXPOSED EDGES ON LID. The side edge-bandings are glued on with masking tape as the clamps, and the front edging is attached with biscuits. All the edging is trimmed flush with a block plane and cleaned up with sandpaper.

SOFT LANDING FOR FINGERS. After gluing on the front edging and trimming it flush with the plywood, rout a cove along the bottom edge to serve as a finger pull.

also masks any minor unevenness at the joints. You can't chamfer the ends now, because the pieces aren't cut to final length, but you should chamfer the edges and pre-finish the pieces.

Frame-and-panel assemblies

The front and exposed side of this built-in are covered with applied frame-and-panel assemblies made from solid walnut and ¼-in.-thick plywood and assembled with simple joinery (see drawings, pp. 112–114).

Base and crown moldings

Like the face frames, both the base and crown molding are solid walnut. For efficiency, mill up both at the same time. The base molding has a simple beveled profile. It's a good idea to leave it a bit wider than its finished size and trim it to fit after installation. The crown molding also is simple.

Install from the Ground Up

BASE: SET IT AND FORGET IT. Installing the cabinets over a separate base makes leveling easy. Assemble the base from scrap plywood, using nails or screws; set it in place and level it. Once that's done, you know that all the cabinets above will be level.

ADD FEET. Use shims to get the base perfectly level and up to the target height. Once the base is at the target height, screw on the plywood feet.

Screw in the Lower Cabinet

1 PUT THE CABINET ON THE BASE. Screw it to the base and to the wall with finish-head screws. Shim behind the cabinet if the wall isn't plumb.

2 SIDE PANEL IS NEXT. Scribe the rear stile to the wall and trim the panel flush with the front of the cabinet. Screw it to the cabinet from inside.

3 TOP IT OFF. Place the fixed back panel on top and screw it to the lower cabinet from above. The screws will be hidden by the upper lockers.

All four bevel cuts are made with the tablesaw blade at 42°. Clean up any saw marks with a handplane or sandpaper. The miters and scribing are done during installation. To support the crown, I use a beveled plywood strip screwed to the top of the case. Cut the strip and bevel its edge.

Last, the lift lid

The top of the lower cabinet features a lift lid, a fixed back (on which the upper cabinets will sit), and two pieces of side trim. I decided to use ¾-in.-thick walnut plywood for the lid and fixed back to eliminate any wood movement

worries. To ensure a good grain match, cut the fixed back and lid from one piece of plywood.

Assembly: Start with a level foundation

Built-in cabinetry must be installed level and plumb, no matter how out of whack the floors and walls may be. One of my favorite tricks is to install a separate base that can be leveled without moving the entire cabinet back and forth in the process. Once the base is complete, install the

Upper Cases: Anchor and Scribe

1 **CLAMP AND SCREW.** Set the four locker cabinets in place and attach one to the next with countersunk drywall screws, which help draw the pieces together. Screw the cabinets to the wall, shimming the back where necessary to keep them plumb.

2 **SCRIBE TO THE WALL.** Where the frames meet the wall, you need to create a seamless fit. The best approach is to set the panel in place and slide a light-colored pencil (which shows on the dark walnut) along the wall to mark its contours.

3 **TRIM TO FIT.** Trim up to the line using a block plane, jigsaw, or belt sander. Your other goal is a flush surface at the front of the cabinet. Next, the side and front panels are screwed on from inside. If you don't like seeing screw heads inside the lockers, cover them with matching maple screw caps, available from Fastcap®.

cases, starting with the lower cabinet and finishing with the upper lockers.

Cover up the plywood edges

Now it's time to install the front frame-and-panel assembly, the lid, the face frames, and the moldings. The front is screwed to the lower case from the inside. The lid is attached to the fixed back with a piano hinge.

When gluing and nailing on the face-frame pieces, attach the verticals first and the horizontals last. Because they're for alignment only, you need only one spline per vertical piece, even though the three middle pieces cover two cabinet sides.

On the horizontal frame pieces, remember to chamfer the ends, and apply finish to that small chamfer before installation.

Now all you have to do is install the crown molding and base molding. Once you're finished, you'll have a handy place to store all sorts of stuff, and a convenient seat where you can put on and take off shoes and boots.

Tony O'Malley, a woodworker in Emmaus, Pa., specializes in making custom built-ins. Illustrations by Bob La Pointe.

Final Details: Lid, Face Frames, and Moldings

1 HINGE THE LID. Once the upper lockers are in place, you're near the finish line. All that's left is to install the lid, the face frames, and the crown and base moldings. To install the lid, screw the piano hinge to the lid, then attach the assembly to the fixed back.

2 FACE FRAMES WITHOUT FRUSTRATION. Rather than attaching a preassembled frame, O'Malley glues and nails on the pieces one at a time, beginning with the verticals. Then he fits the horizontals.

3 THE TOPPER. To give a better attachment surface for the crown molding, nail on a plywood support piece along the edges (top). Then miter the crown, and glue and nail it in place (above). Don't hurry any of these final jobs, because these details are the most visible. Conceal the nail heads with a colored wax crayon.

STANLEY®

GARAGES & OUTDOOR SPACES

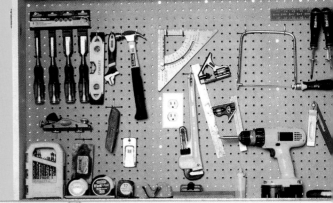

Quick and Sturdy Utility Shelves

BY DAVID SCHIFF Looking for sturdy shelving that's inexpensive and quick and easy to build? All you need is a pile of 2×4s and a sheet of CDX plywood—a sturdy grade of plywood that's most commonly used for house sheathing. The shelves are 48 in. long to make efficient use of the plywood sheet. You can easily adapt the plan to fit your space by making the unit shorter or changing the depth of the shelves. And if you have lots of stuff to store, it won't take much more time to assemble two or three of these while you are at it.

David Schiff is an editorial project manager, writer, and editor with extensive experience in the areas of home improvement, construction, and woodworking. He is the author of the *Stanley Quick Guide to Garage Storage Solutions,* and his upcoming book *Built-Ins and Storage* will be available in Spring 2016. Photos by the author. Illustrations by Mario Ferro.

UTILITY SHELVES

WHAT YOU'LL NEED

- 5 shelves, ³⁄₄ in. × 16 in. × 48 in.
- 10 long rails, 1¹⁄₂ in. × 1¹⁄₂ in. × 48 in.
- 10 side rails, 1¹⁄₂ in. × 1¹⁄₂ in. × 13 in.
- 4 stiles, 1¹⁄₂ in. × 3¹⁄₂ in. × 77 in.

- 4 bottom spacers, 1¹⁄₂ in. × 3¹⁄₂ in. × 6 in.
- 16 spacers, 1¹⁄₂ in. × 3¹⁄₂ in. × 15 in.
- 2¹⁄₂-in. all-purpose screws
- 1¹⁄₄-in. all-purpose screws

TIP If you are making more than one shelving unit, save time by cutting parts for all the units at one time.

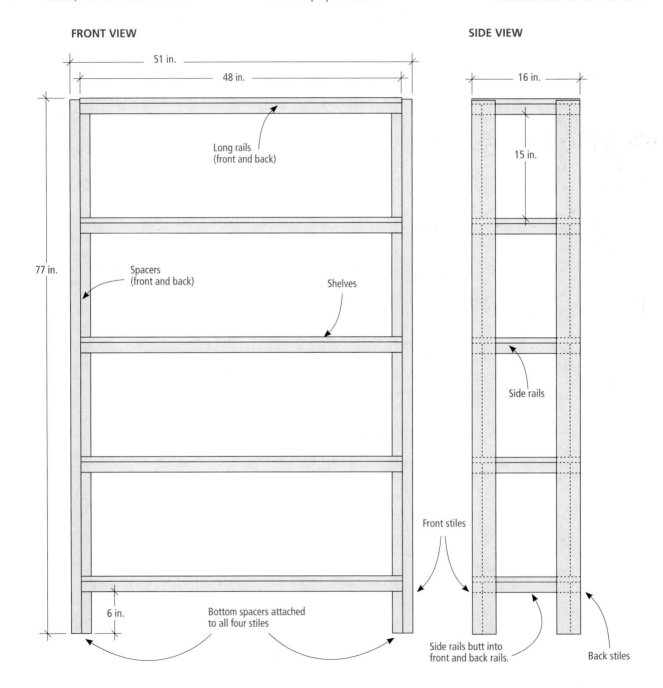

FRONT VIEW

51 in.

48 in.

Long rails (front and back)

77 in.

Spacers (front and back)

Shelves

6 in.

Bottom spacers attached to all four stiles

SIDE VIEW

16 in.

15 in.

Side rails

Front stiles

Side rails butt into front and back rails.

Back stiles

1 **CUT THE PLYWOOD.** Put the plywood for the shelves on the floor with scraps of plywood underneath and lay out the first crosscut at 16 in. Set the blade on your circular saw to cut through the plywood and into the scrap without cutting into the floor. Lay out and cut the rest of the shelves.

2 **CROSSCUT THE LUMBER PARTS TO LENGTH.** When cutting four or five boards to the same length, clamp them together flush at the ends and make each cut in one pass.

TIP If you don't have a tablesaw to rip the rails, you can purchase 8-ft. 2×2s (actual size 1½ in. by 1½ in.) at a lumberyard or home center.

PREDRILLING

When securing a 1½-in. by 1½-in. rail to a spacer, predrill the hole to prevent splitting the end of the rail. You may want to predrill all the holes for the 2½-in. screws, just to make it easier to drive them. To select the right size drill bit, hold the screw behind the bit—if you can see the screw threads but not the body of the screw, you have the right bit.

3 **RIP THE RAILS TO WIDTH.** Use a tablesaw to rip all the 48-in. pieces and all the 13-in. pieces into 1½-in. by 1½-in. rails. Be sure to use a push stick when making these cuts.

1 **ATTACH THE BOTTOM SPACERS.** All the lumber connections are made with 2½-in. screws. Attach a bottom spacer to each stile with two screws. Use a clamp to help hold the spacer in position while you drive the screws.

2 **ATTACH A LONG RAIL.** Place two stiles on edge and position a long rail between. Attach with two screws on each end—one through the stile and one into the bottom spacer.

3 **ATTACH A SIDE RAIL.** Put a side rail in place butting into the long rail and secure it with one screw through the stile and one into the bottom spacer.

4 **ADD THE SECOND BOTTOM RAIL.** Stand up the stile/rail assembly you made and clamp it to the side of your workbench, or have a helper hold it upright. Put the other two stiles and a long rail in place. Screw the side rails to the bottom spacers and stiles.

5 **INSTALL THE LOWEST SHELF.** Put a shelf in place and attach it to the rails with 1¼-in. screws spaced about every 6 in.

6 **ADD SPACERS AND COMPLETE THE UNIT.** At each corner, put a spacer down against the shelf and secure it to the stiles with four 2½-in. screws. Repeat the process for adding rails, shelves, and spacers until the unit is complete.

COMMERCIAL WALL-STORAGE SYSTEMS

Getting stuff off the floor and up on the wall is an essential part of any garage storage scheme. There are lots of wall systems you can buy to help you achieve this goal. You'll find hooks designed to hold various items—from garden hoses to garden tools to bicycles or ladders. There are metal grids to which you attach various hooks, baskets, and shelves at different heights.

If you want the option of easily changing your wall storage layout, channels are a great way to go because hooks, baskets, and shelves can be snapped in or removed in seconds. Some channel systems are designed to cover whole walls. Or you can purchase individual lengths of channel. The channel system shown here uses 48-in.-long channels. The end caps are sold separately, so you can line up the channels for lengths in any 48-in. increment. You screw the channels into studs, and then you snap in the accessories of your choice.

Overhead
Garage Storage

BY DAVID SCHIFF ▇ This storage rack, constructed of 2×4s and plywood, is a great way to gain storage while sacrificing zero floor space. It is extremely sturdy thanks to the use of lag screws, joist hangers, and L-angles.

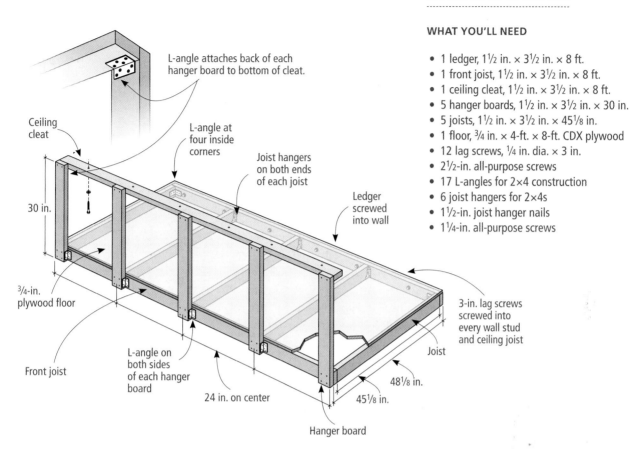

L-angle attaches back of each hanger board to bottom of cleat.

Ceiling cleat

L-angle at four inside corners

Joist hangers on both ends of each joist

Ledger screwed into wall

30 in.

¾-in. plywood floor

Front joist

L-angle on both sides of each hanger board

24 in. on center

Hanger board

Joist

3-in. lag screws screwed into every wall stud and ceiling joist

48⅛ in.

45⅛ in.

OVERHEAD STORAGE

WHAT YOU'LL NEED

- 1 ledger, 1½ in. × 3½ in. × 8 ft.
- 1 front joist, 1½ in. × 3½ in. × 8 ft.
- 1 ceiling cleat, 1½ in. × 3½ in. × 8 ft.
- 5 hanger boards, 1½ in. × 3½ in. × 30 in.
- 5 joists, 1½ in. × 3½ in. × 45⅛ in.
- 1 floor, ¾ in. × 4-ft. × 8-ft. CDX plywood
- 12 lag screws, ¼ in. dia. × 3 in.
- 2½-in. all-purpose screws
- 17 L-angles for 2×4 construction
- 6 joist hangers for 2×4s
- 1½-in. joist hanger nails
- 1¼-in. all-purpose screws

The simple design is easily adapted to many garage situations. The 30-in.-deep version shown here is installed in a garage with a 10-ft. ceiling, leaving plenty of room to walk beneath. If your ceiling is lower, you can make a shallower unit, or you can reduce the width or length to suit as long as you space the joists 4 ft. or less on center.

David Schiff is an editorial project manager, writer, and editor with extensive experience in the areas of home improvement, construction, and woodworking. He is the author of the *Stanley Quick Guide to Garage Storage Solutions,* and his upcoming book *Built-Ins and Storage* will be available in Spring 2016. Photos by the author. Illustrations by Mario Ferro.

TIP A full sheet of plywood is used for the floor of this overhead storage rack. If you don't have a way to transport 4-ft.-wide sheets, have the lumberyard or home center cut the sheet in half along its length. The seam won't matter in the finished project.

1 **LAY OUT JOIST AND HANGER BOARD POSITIONS.** Clamp three 8-ft. 2×4s together, edges up and ends flush. Starting from your left, strike lines at 23¼ in., 47¼ in., and 71¼ in. Make an X to the right of each line. On two of those boards, extend the lines and Xs to one face; label these boards as the ledger and the front joist. Extend the lines to the other face of the front joist. Label the third board as the ceiling cleat.

2 LAY OUT THE LEDGER. Use a 4-ft. level to draw an 8-ft.-long level line along the wall 30 in. from the ceiling.

3 FIND THE STUDS ALONG THE LINE. If your garage isn't painted, you can easily identify stud locations by the vertical rows of nails or screws. Otherwise, use a stud finder to mark where your layout line crosses each stud.

4 POSITION THE LEDGER. With a helper holding one end, align the bottom of the ledger to the layout line with the X marks to your left. Drive a 2½-in. screw through the ledger into the stud closest to one end of the board. Check for level, and then drive a screw into the stud closest to the other end.

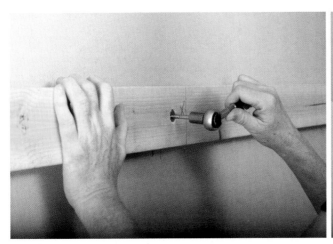

5 SECURE THE LEDGER. Predrill and install one lag screw with washer into each stud along the length of the ledger. If a screw falls over an X, you'll need to counterbore the screw hole so the screw head will be below the surface where it won't interfere with the joist. Make the counterbore with a ¾-in. spade bit, then predrill the screw hole through the counterbore.

6 LAY OUT THE CEILING CLEAT. Use a 4-ft. level to make a plumb mark on the ceiling above each end of the ledger. Use a framing square to make a line on the ceiling square to each end. Then use a chalkline to extend these lines 48⅛ in. from each end. (That extra ⅛ in. will make it easier to slide the plywood floor into place.) Snap a line parallel to the wall between the ends of the two lines. Use a stud finder to mark where the line crosses joists in the ceiling.

7 **INSTALL THE CEILING CLEAT.** With a helper, align the ceiling cleat to the inside of the line, with the Xs to your right as you face the wall. Hold the cleat in place with a screw into a joist at each end. Predrill, and then install one lag screw into each joist.

8 **CUT AND INSTALL THE HANGER BOARDS.** Using a circular saw or power miter saw, cut the five hanger boards to length. Position each along its layout line, covering the X and butting into the ceiling, then attach it to the cleat with a 2½-in. screw. Check for plumb, and then add a second screw.

9 **INSTALL L-ANGLES WHERE CLEAT MEETS HANGERS.** Use an L-angle with 1¼-in. screws to attach the back face of each hanger board to the bottom of the ceiling cleat.

WHAT IF THE JOISTS RUN PARALLEL TO THE CEILING CLEAT?

This project assumes that the ceiling joists in your garage run perpendicular to the ceiling cleat. If the joists run parallel to the cleat, you have two choices: You can adjust the width of the storage unit to the nearest joist. Or you can make five 2×4 cross-cleats to span two joists. Use 3-in. lag screws to attach the cross-cleats through the ceiling into the joists. Then lag-screw the ceiling cleat to the cross-cleats.

10 **INSTALL THE JOIST HANGERS.** Using 1½-in. joist hanger nails, install three joist hangers on the ledger and three on the front joist positioned so that the joist ends will cover the X at the three inner layout lines. It's important to install the hangers before you install the front joist because the hanger boards are not yet stable enough to hammer against. Use a scrap of 2×4 as shown to make sure the hangers are properly positioned.

11 **INSTALL THE OUTER L-ANGLES.** Strike a line 1½ in. from each end of the ledger (the thickness of each joist) and the front joist. Install an L-angle at each end of the ledger and the front joist.

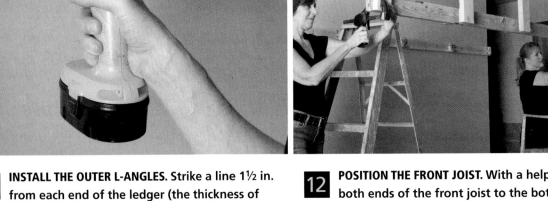

12 **POSITION THE FRONT JOIST.** With a helper, align both ends of the front joist to the bottom outside edges of the outermost hanger joists and then clamp the joist in place.

13 **ATTACH THE FRONT JOIST.** Clamp the front joist to another hanger board. Check that the front joist is level and then make the connection with four 2½-in. screws. Clamp and then screw each connection.

14 **INSTALL THE JOISTS.** Cut the five joists to 45⅛ in. long. Then slip three of the joists into their joist hangers and secure them with 1½-in. joist hanger nails into the angled hole on each side of each joist hanger. Put the outer joists against the L-angles and secure with 1¼-in. screws.

15 INSTALL THE REMAINING L-ANGLES. Use L-angles and 1¼-in. screws to secure each side of each hanger board to the front joist.

16 INSTALL THE FLOOR. Put the plywood in place, climb aboard, and snap lines to locate the joists below at 24 in., 48 in., and 72 in. Secure the plywood with 1¼-in. screws about every 12 in. into the ledger, front joist, and joists.

HOIST IT OUT OF THE WAY

There are several methods available for stowing bulky items like bikes or ladders in the garage. There are simple ceiling hooks and wall hooks, overhead racks for ladders, and even a "claw" for bikes. You screw the claw to the ceiling and it grabs the rim when you bump a wheel against it.

A hoist is a convenient way to get moderately heavy stuff up out of the way without having to muscle it over your head. You'll find hoists designed for bikes and very similar systems designed for ladders, kayaks, or canoes.

A Customizable Garden Tool Rack

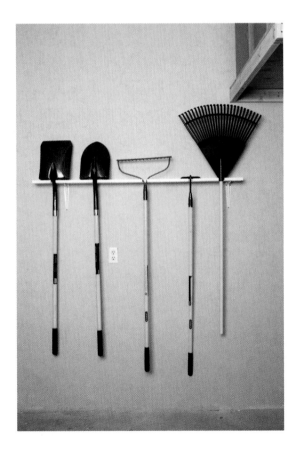

BY DAVID SCHIFF In less than an hour, you can get that jumble of long-handled yard tools neatly stored in this simple rack. The best part is the rack will be customized to exactly the tools you want to store. You can place it at any convenient height, as long as there is enough room for the tool handles to hang below. All you need is a length of 1×6 lumber, two 5-in. by 6-in. metal brackets, six 1¼-in. screws, and two ⅝-in. screws.

David Schiff is an editorial project manager, writer, and editor with extensive experience in the areas of home improvement, construction, and woodworking. He is the author of the *Stanley Quick Guide to Garage Storage Solutions,* and his upcoming book *Built-Ins and Storage* will be available in Spring 2016. Photos by the author.

1 **DECIDE ON THE LENGTH.** Lay your long-handled garden tools side by side with about 2 in. clearance separating each tool from the next. Measuring across the point where the handle meets each tool, determine the distance from the middle of one handle to the middle of the next and write down these measurements.

2 **CUT THE RACK TO LENGTH AND LAY OUT THE HOLES.** Add 12 in. to the sum of your handle measurements and cut a 1×6 to that length. Use a combination square to draw a line along the length of the board, ¾ in. from one edge. Mark 6 in. along that line for the first tool and then make marks for the rest of the tool handles, adding 6 in. to each measurement you noted.

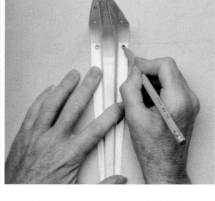

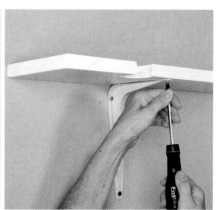

3 **DRILL THE TOOL HOLES.** Clamp the board to your bench with at least 2 in. overhanging along the length. Center a 2-in. hole saw over each mark and drill a hole. The saw will overlap the edge of the board, creating a slot for the handles. If you want to paint or finish the rack board, now is the time to do it.

4 **INSTALL THE BRACKETS.** Use a 4-ft. level to draw a line on the wall at your chosen height. Find the two studs that fall closest to where you want the ends of your rack to be (see "Find the studs along the line" on p. 128). Center the brackets over the studs and with the line passing through the top holes of each bracket's long leg. Mark for the screw holes. Predrill and then attach the brackets with 1¼-in. screws.

5 **ATTACH THE RACK.** Center the rack across the brackets, adjusting if necessary to prevent a slot from falling over a bracket. Mark for screw holes. Take the rack down to predrill and then secure it to the bracket with ⅝-in. screws.

> **TIP** When using a hole saw, drill just until the pilot bit comes through the other side. Then flip the board, put the pilot bit in the pilot hole, and finish the cut. You'll get a cleaner cut, and the waste piece won't get stuck in the hole saw.

Fold-up Worktable/ Tool Cabinet

BY DAVID SCHIFF ▮ You long for a convenient workstation with a good-size table, a place with your tools and fasteners organized and right at hand. But you still need to get your car in the garage. Here's the solution. This project features a fold-up worktable with peg-board above and a cabinet below. Open the doors, slip on the removable feet, drop the table, and you have a rock-solid work surface. Close it up, and every

FOLD-UP WORKTABLE

WHAT YOU'LL NEED

- 2 side furring, $\frac{3}{4}$ in. × $2\frac{1}{2}$ in. × $25\frac{1}{4}$ in., pine
- 2 top and bottom furring, $\frac{3}{4}$ in. × $2\frac{1}{2}$ in. × 43 in., pine
- 2 middle furring, $\frac{3}{4}$ in. × $2\frac{1}{2}$ in. × $20\frac{1}{4}$ in., pine
- 1 pegboard, $25\frac{1}{4}$ in. × 48 in.
- 2 sides, $\frac{3}{4}$ in. × $5\frac{1}{2}$ in. × 61 in., pine
- 1 top, $\frac{3}{4}$ in. × $5\frac{1}{2}$ in. × 48 in., pine
- 1 pegboard bottom, $1\frac{1}{2}$ in. × $5\frac{1}{2}$ in. × 48 in., pine
- 1 center post, $\frac{3}{4}$ in. × $5\frac{1}{2}$ in. × $33\frac{1}{2}$ in., pine
- 7 shelves, $\frac{3}{4}$ in. × $5\frac{1}{2}$ in. × $23\frac{5}{8}$ in., pine
- 8 dividers, $\frac{3}{4}$ in. × $5\frac{1}{2}$ in. × $7\frac{1}{4}$ in., pine
- 6 dividers, $\frac{3}{4}$ in. × $5\frac{1}{2}$ in. × $9\frac{15}{16}$ in., pine
- 4 bottom shelf cleats, $\frac{3}{4}$ in. × $5\frac{1}{2}$ in. × $1\frac{1}{2}$ in., pine
- 2 stiles, $\frac{3}{4}$ in. × $1\frac{1}{2}$ in. × $34\frac{1}{4}$ in., pine
- 2 doors, $\frac{3}{4}$ in. × $23\frac{1}{8}$ in. × $32\frac{3}{4}$ in., plywood
- 1 worktable, $\frac{3}{4}$ in. × $25\frac{1}{4}$ in. × 48 in., plywood
- 2 door foot bottoms, $\frac{3}{4}$ in. × $2\frac{1}{4}$ in. × 5 in., plywood
- 4 door foot sides, $\frac{3}{4}$ in. × $1\frac{1}{2}$ in. × 5 in., plywood
- 2 levelers, $\frac{3}{4}$ in. × 5 in. × 5 in., plywood
- 2 side table edging, $\frac{3}{4}$ in. × $\frac{3}{4}$ in. × $25\frac{1}{4}$ in.
- 1 front table edging, $\frac{3}{4}$ in. × $\frac{3}{4}$ in. × $49\frac{1}{2}$ in.
- 1 table cleat, $\frac{3}{4}$ in. × 10 in. × 45 in., plywood
- 4 hinges, $\frac{3}{4}$ in. × $2\frac{1}{2}$ in.
- 1 continuous hinge, 48 in.
- 2 hooks and eyes, $2\frac{1}{2}$ in.
- 1 swivel hasp, $4\frac{1}{2}$ in.
- $1\frac{1}{4}$-in. screws
- $1\frac{1}{2}$-in. screws
- $2\frac{1}{4}$-in. screws
- $2\frac{1}{2}$-in. screws
- 4d finish nails
- 8d finish nails

TIP Wood can easily split when you drive screws close to ends and edges. To prevent splitting, drive the screws just flush; don't bury them. Predrilling holes also helps.

FRONT VIEW   Table and doors not shown

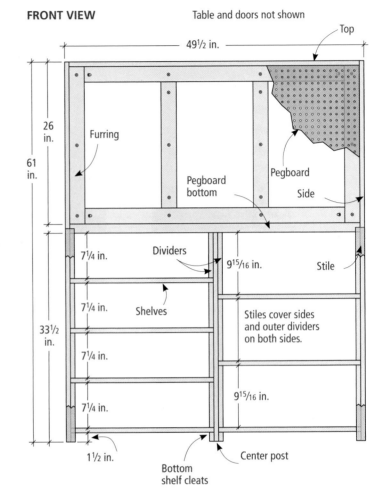

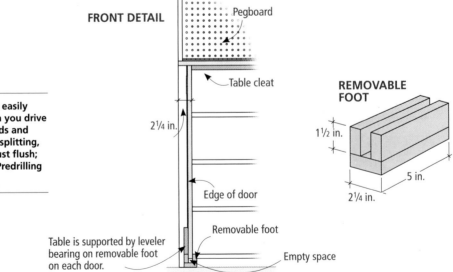

FRONT DETAIL

REMOVABLE FOOT

Table is supported by leveler bearing on removable foot on each door.

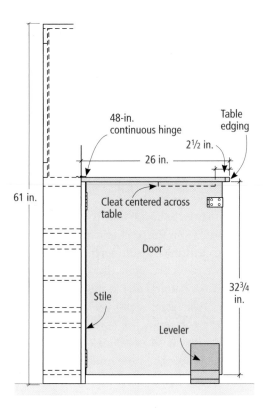

48-in. continuous hinge

Table edging

2½ in.

26 in.

61 in.

Cleat centered across table

Door

Stile

32¾ in.

Leveler

thing is hidden and protected in a unit that protrudes just 7 in. from the wall.

This worktable/tool cabinet is built from AC plywood. Use the clear "A" side for the faces of the doors and the work surface of the table. The shelves and trim pieces are #2 pine, which has some knots. The worktable is protected with two coats of wipe-on polyurethane.

Install the shelves

The 1×6 shelves will butt into each side of the cabinet and the center post and will be positioned and supported by the 1×6 dividers. Cut the center post to fit between the 2×6 pegboard bottom and the floor. Cut the seven shelves, the eight left-hand dividers, and the six right-hand dividers to the lengths in the parts list. For quick accuracy, make the cuts using stops on a power miter saw. Otherwise, a circular saw will do fine.

David Schiff is an editorial project manager, writer, and editor with extensive experience in the areas of home improvement, construction, and woodworking. He is the author of the *Stanley Quick Guide to Garage Storage Solutions,* and his upcoming book *Built-Ins and Storage* will be available in Spring 2016. Photos by the author. Illustrations by Mario Ferro.

MAKE A CROSSCUTTING JIG FOR A CIRCULAR SAW

Start with a piece of ¼-in. plywood base that's 48 in. long and at least 6 in. wider than the base of your saw. Glue and clamp a ¾-in. by 6-in. by 52-in. plywood guide flush to the outside edge of the base and overhanging about 2 in. on each side. When the glue dries, clamp the jig to your bench with enough of the base overhanging so that you can run your circular saw along the guide, trimming the base. To use the jig, clamp or screw it to the sacrificial piece with the trimmed edge of the jig base at the cutline on the workpiece.

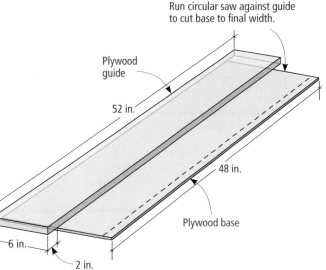

Run circular saw against guide to cut base to final width.

Plywood guide

52 in.

48 in.

Plywood base

6 in.

2 in.

Install the Pegboard and Frame

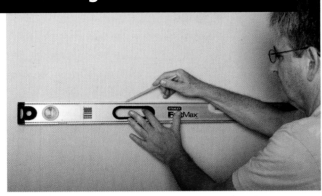

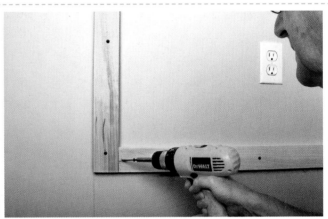

1 LOCATE THE PEGBOARD AND FURRING. Find the center of the stud nearest to where you want to locate the left side of the pegboard (see "Find the studs along the line" on p. 128). Then find the centers of the next three studs to the right. To locate the left side of the pegboard, measure 1¼ in. to the left of the center of the stud. Use a 4-ft. level to make a plumb line from the floor up to 60¼ in. Draw another plumb line 48 in. to the right to locate the right side of the pegboard. Connect the top of the lines with a level line for the top of the pegboard.

2 CUT AND ATTACH THE FURRING. The pegboard is "furred out" from the wall to allow room for the tool hangers. Cut the outside furring strips to the dimensions in the parts list, then attach them with 2½-in. screws. Next, cut and install the horizontal furring strips with 2½-in. screws every 6 in. into studs. To catch the studs, toe-screw the horizontal strips into the side vertical strips as shown. Finally, cut and install two middle vertical strips centered over the studs.

3 CUT THE PEGBOARD. Use a circular saw with a jig to crosscut the pegboard to 25¼ in. Put the pegboard on the floor with a sacrificial piece of ply-wood underneath and lay out a crosscut at 25¼ in. Set the blade on your circular saw to cut through the pegboard and into the sacrificial piece without cutting into the floor.

4 INSTALL THE PEGBOARD. Attach the pegboard to the furring strips with 1¼-in. screws into the corners and every six holes along the perimeter and the middle strips.

5 **CUT AND INSTALL THE SIDES AND TOP.** Cut the sides to the dimensions in the parts list. Attach them to the side furring strips with 1¼-in. screws. Cut the top to fit between the sides and attach it with two screws through each side and screws down into the furring.

6 **CUT AND ATTACH THE 2X6 PEGBOARD BOTTOM.** Cut a piece of 2×6 to 48 in. With a helper holding it in place, attach the piece with 2½-in. screws up into the furring and then drive two screws through each side.

EXTEND AN OUTLET

What if the pegboard covers an electrical outlet? Lucky you! It's handy to have power at your workstation. All you need is a box extender. Turn off power to the outlet. Take off the cover plate and measure to locate one corner of the box. Trace the extender on the pegboard. Cut the hole with a saber saw. Pull the receptacle through the hole before you attach the pegboard. Slip the extender over the receptacle, and secure the receptacle through the extender with the longer screws provided. Replace the cover.

1 **INSTALL THE CENTER POST.** Put two shelves up against the bottom of the 2×6 with the center post fitted between. This will position the center post while you secure it with two 2½-in. screws through the 2×6. Then remove the shelves.

2 **INSTALL THE LEFT-HAND SHELVES AND DIVIDERS.** Install a pair of short dividers with four 1¼-in. screws, clamp a shelf in place, and secure it with two 2¼-in. screws on each end. Repeat for all four left-hand shelves and their dividers. Extend lines around the outside of the cabinet as you go to ensure that your screws don't miss the shelves.

3 **INSTALL THE RIGHT-HAND SHELVES.** Install the top two right-hand shelves and their dividers as you did on the left, but this time use 2½-in. screws through the left-hand dividers and the center post into the shelves.

4 **INSTALL THE FINAL SHELF.** You won't have access to the inside end of the last shelf, so predrill holes for toe-screws into the divider and secure with 1½-in. screws as shown.

5 **CUT AND INSTALL THE BOTTOM SHELF CLEATS.** For both ends of both bottom shelves, scribe cuts on pieces of 1×6 to fit snugly underneath. Cut the pieces and tap them into place with a hammer. No need for fasteners or glue.

6 **CUT AND INSTALL THE STILES.** Rip pine to 1½ in. wide for the stiles and cut them to reach from the floor to ¾ in. below the top of the 2×6. Install them with glue and 8d finish nails.

1 **CUT THE DOORS AND WORK-TABLE.** Check your door dimensions—they may vary a bit from the dimensions in the parts list. For the height of the doors, measure from the bottom of the shelves to the top of the stiles. For the width, measure between the inside of the stiles, divide in half, and subtract ¹⁄₁₆ in. for each door. Using the same technique as for the pegboard, crosscut a plywood sheet to the door height. Rip the doors to final width on the table-saw or with the circular saw and jig. Then crosscut the worktable to 25¼ in.

2 **MARK THE HINGE LOCATIONS.** On the face of the doors, mark hinge locations 2 in. from the top and bottom. Put each door in position and shim it flush to the top of the stiles. Then transfer the hinge locations onto the stiles.

3 **SCRIBE THE MORTISES.** Scribe the outline of each hinge mortise on the outside edge of each door and the inside of the stiles. Set a combination square to the thickness of a hinge leaf and use it to scribe the mortise depth on the faces of the stiles and doors.

4 **CUT THE MORTISES AND INSTALL THE DOORS.** Chop the sides of the mortises and then slice them out to depth. Attach the hinges to the doors and then to the stiles.

TIP When chopping mortises, place the chisel on the scribe line with the flat side toward the outside of the mortise. Tap the chisel with a mallet or hammer until it cuts to the scribed hinge depth.

5 **MAKE THE DOOR FEET.** The removable door feet supply solid bearing for the worktable when it is supported by the open doors. When not in use, you can stow them in the cabinet. Cut the foot base and sides to the dimensions in the parts list. Assemble each foot with glue and a clamp, placing the sides flush to the edges of the base.

TIP It's a good idea to protect the working surface of the worktable with a couple of coats of polyure- thane. You can brush it on or, easier, use the wipe-on variety.

6 **INSTALL THE FOOT LEVELERS.** The levelers compen- sate for any irregularity in the level of your garage floor. Cut them to the dimensions in the parts list. At the bottom of each door face, make a mark ½ in. in from the outside edge. Open a door until it is perpendicular to the 2×6—use a framing square to check. Put a foot in place, put glue on the back of the leveler, and push the edge of the leveler firmly against the foot as you clamp the leveler in place. Now, even if your garage floor isn't level, the door feet will fit snugly under the levelers, firmly supporting the worktable.

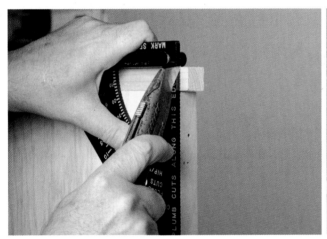

7 **INSTALL THE TABLE EDGING.** Use a utility knife and square to scribe cuts in place as shown. First, cut the side edging pieces so that they will fit flush with the front and back of the worktable. Install the pieces with glue and 4d finish nails. Cut the front edging to cover the ends of the side edging and install with glue and nails.

8 **INSTALL THE CONTINUOUS HINGE.** Put the table- top in place on the open doors with the feet in place. Center the continuous hinge over where the tabletop abuts the 2×6 pegboard bottom. Predrill and screw the hinge in place.

9 INSTALL HOOKS AND EYES. Install an eye on each side edge of the tabletop, then raise the table-top and insert the hook into the eye to locate where to screw in the hook. Attach the hooks.

10 MARK THE POSITION OF THE WORKTABLE CLEAT. The cleat stiffens the worktable and provides stops for the doors. Open the doors square to the cabinet. Scribe lines where the inside of the doors meets the bottom of the worktable.

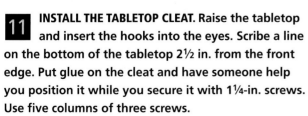

11 INSTALL THE TABLETOP CLEAT. Raise the tabletop and insert the hooks into the eyes. Scribe a line on the bottom of the tabletop 2½ in. from the front edge. Put glue on the cleat and have someone help you position it while you secure it with 1¼-in. screws. Use five columns of three screws.

12 INSTALL THE SWIVEL HASP AND SMOOTH EDGES. A swivel hasp is a sturdy latch that will allow you to padlock the cabinet if you wish. Position it 3 in. from the top of the door and install with the screws provided. Round exposed edges of the project, especially the plywood, to prevent splinters.

A Small and Stylish Outdoor Shed

BY JOHN MICHAEL DAVIS When my clients asked me to design a small outdoor storage shed for their potting equipment, I saw it as a fun project that would be complicated only by New Orleans's balmy, wood-attacking climate. To keep their little shed from succumbing to the elements, I used a series of techniques I've developed in my 30 years as a New Orleans restoration carpenter.

The first line of defense is a sturdy frame built with ACQ pressure-treated stock that has a 0.60 retention level. Most folks don't realize it, but pressure-treated lumber is available in treatment levels from 0.15 to 0.60. The numbers translate to the amount of treatment chemical (in pounds) per cubic foot of lumber. Higher numbers mean more resistance to insects and decay.

Stainless-steel fasteners are used throughout, and Enkamat® (www.colbond-usa.com) drainage mats between the frame and the siding prevent rot and mold from getting a foothold. I capped the little structure with slate roofing I bought from a salvage dealer. Louvered doors and bronze screening over a pair of soffit vents provide lots of ventilation, which prevents the objects inside from mildewing.

My clients wanted a small shed, but you could easily adapt the design to match the scale of your outdoor living space. Unless you're willing to spend several hundred dollars for custom shutters, I'd start the design process with stock shutters or louvered doors.

John Michael Davis is a restoration carpenter in New Orleans. Photos by the author. Illustration by John Hartman.

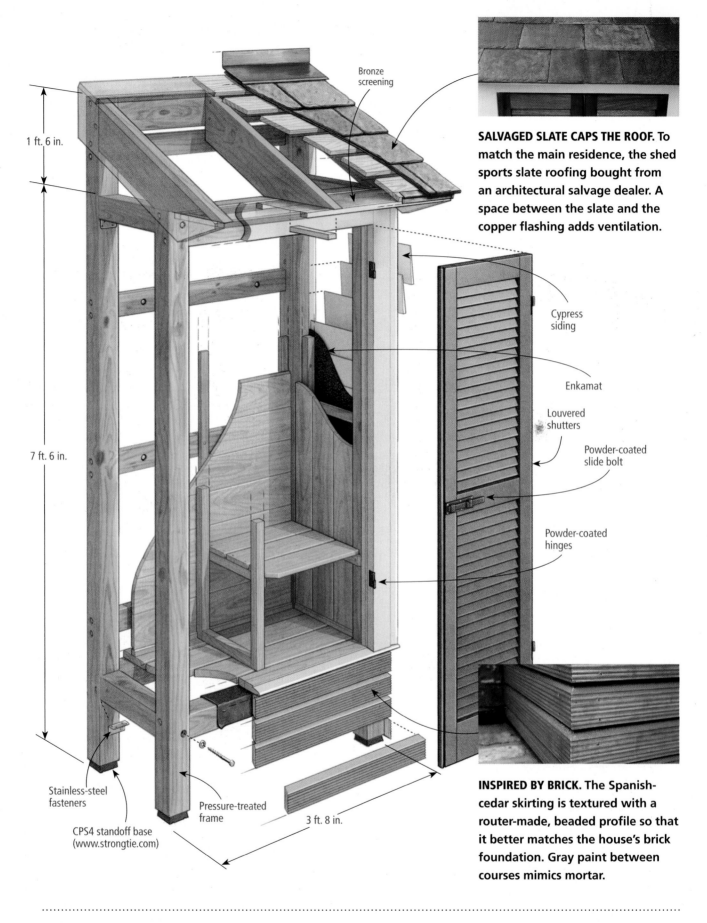

Bronze screening

SALVAGED SLATE CAPS THE ROOF. To match the main residence, the shed sports slate roofing bought from an architectural salvage dealer. A space between the slate and the copper flashing adds ventilation.

1 ft. 6 in.

7 ft. 6 in.

Cypress siding

Enkamat

Louvered shutters

Powder-coated slide bolt

Powder-coated hinges

Stainless-steel fasteners

CPS4 standoff base (www.strongtie.com)

Pressure-treated frame

3 ft. 8 in.

INSPIRED BY BRICK. The Spanish-cedar skirting is textured with a router-made, beaded profile so that it better matches the house's brick foundation. Gray paint between courses mimics mortar.